How To Plant A Vegetable Garden

By Derek Fell

Distributed by

CURRENT, INC.

Derek Fell, author, poses with a 312 lb. pumpkin.

About the Author

Derek Fell is director of both the *National Garden Bureau* — an information office sponsored by the American garden seed industry — and *All-America Selections* — the national seed trials.

His latest assignment was to write a position paper for the White House as part of a Garden Group Task Force, to advise the President how gardening and home food production could help fight inflation.

He began his working life as a newspaper reporter in England, and after two years on the news desk of a rural weekly newspaper he joined an advertising agency in London, specializing in promoting horticultural products. He helped Jan de Graaff, the American lily hybridizer, introduce his hybrid lilies in Great Britain, and he also worked with Europe's biggest wholesale seed house, Hurst, on its publicity programs.

After seven years promoting horticultural products in Great Britain he moved to America to edit American garden seed catalogs, and to help launch new vegetables including the *Golden* Beet, *Pixie Hybrid* Tomato and *Green Arrow* Pea.

Over the past several years he has appeared on television talk shows discussing gardening from seed. He lectures and writes extensively for newspapers and magazines about vegetable gardening, and he is a contributor to *Encyclopaedia Britannica.*

For the *National Garden Bureau* he writes a garden page distributed to more than 5,000 news media, including newspapers, magazines, radio and television. In addition, his press releases for *All-America Selections* are read by an estimated audience of 62,000,000 people.

In spite of Fell's ability and a real passion for gardening, his vegetable garden occupies an area just 12 ft. wide by 20 ft. deep. He finds it plenty large enough to grow a bountiful harvest of fresh vegetables from April until December in sufficient quantity to feed a family of four.

It didn't use to be that way. His first serious attempt at vegetable gardening was in a space 50 ft. by 50 ft. He found it to be too large an area to manage efficiently, and made the mistake of most beginner gardeners of trying to plant too much. "When you're retired with all day to spend in the garden, or want to take on a vegetable garden as a full time hobby then 50 ft. by 50 ft. — or even bigger — is fine. But the average family man doesn't have all that time to spend. He wants maximum reward from minimum effort, and enough to feed his family." These thoughts, and 15 years continuous experience of working with vegetables in the seed industry inspired Derek Fell to write this book.

About the Photography

Most of the color pictures in this book were taken by the author of actual fruits and vegetables exactly as nature presented them.

They were shot with a standard Rolleiflex twin-lens reflex camera on Ektachrome film.

The black and white photography is mostly from the files of the *National Garden Bureau*, contributed by a number of garden companies, while the line etchings on pages 38-80 are from antique seed catalogs, representing an engraving art that sadly disappeared with the invention of the camera and less time consuming engraving techniques.

Cover by Jean Helmer
Art by Heather O'Connor

Copyright © 1975 by Countryside Books   A.B. Morse Company
200 James Street   Barrington, Illinois 60010

ISBN 06-465045-6

Contents

4

Six hours full sun each day allows this vegetable garden to return a bountiful harvest in spite of dense woodland on all sides. Ample spacing and a thick straw mulch to smother weeds encourages maximum productivity.

(Above) Youthful gardener straddles a row of bush wax beans, methodically picking over each plant to harvest a pailful of fresh pods.

(Top) Pictured above is a well-planned vegetable garden size 10 ft. by 15 ft. deep, featuring tomatoes, peppers, zucchini squash, cabbage, carrots, lettuce and onions. This size garden and these easy-to-grow, productive varieties are ideal for beginner gardeners.

The True Value
of a Vegetable Garden

In December, 1974 I was invited by the White House to submit recommendations on how gardening and home food production help fight inflation. The first question I sought to answer was whether in fact vegetable gardening can *really* help to fight inflation. Convincing evidence was needed to show that it did and to what extent.

I decided that the most convincing example was to be found in Japan, where a fresh local-grown cantaloupe today costs $10.00 in season. The country has a population density that makes it impossible for the majority of the people to grow their own food in order to combat these high food prices.

Every inch of available land in Japan is already under intensive cultivation or populated, except mountains too steep to farm or build on. Garden space around houses is extremely small or non-existent. Community gardens like we have in America and Europe are out of the question owing to the premium on land.

The inability for most of the Japanese population to fight inflation by not being able to grow their own food is a distressing situation, and it emphasizes how fortunate American families are in having large yards or access to plenty of good land to grow their own food and avoid this kind of catastrophe.

Even a flower garden helps to fight inflation. The more enjoyment people can find at home, the less money and energy they need to spend away from home.

In the Cleveland Public Schools garden program during the 1974 growing season it has been calculated that 21,000 schoolchildren raised over $622,000 worth of fresh vegetables from a cash investment of $15,600 to pay all costs of seeds, plants, equipment, after-care products and instruction materials. In addition to fresh vegetables the youngsters raised 20,000 rows of cut flowers and potted plants for beauty outside and indoors.

Even the smallest size family garden (say 10 ft. by 15 ft.) will grow about $120.00 worth of fresh produce which can be considered direct savings over store-bought vegetables. This figure can be increased if you enlarge the garden and if you like to can or freeze surplus crops from your garden, such as tomatoes, beans, corn, zucchini, Brussels sprouts, and beets.

The more time you spend enjoying your garden the less time you need to spend away from home. That saves on gasoline, eating-out and other away-from-home costs. Once you have your garden started you'll be amazed how much time you *want* to spend in your garden — not how much time the garden *demands* you spend in it.

There are other advantages to vegetable gardening besides the prospect of saving money and fighting inflation.

Compared to other nations of the world (and approved nutritional standards) the percentage of vegetables in the average American diet is extremely low, and nutritionists have been worried about it.

Russian scientists who have been studying the amazing longevity of people in the Caucasus mountain range on the eastern shores of the Black Sea, believe that diet is the most important factor if a person is to live more than 100 years.

The number of people over 100 years of age in this particular region of southern Russia is estimated at 5,000 individuals. The oldest living person in the region is believed to be almost 170 years old, and the Russian scientists feel that it may be possible for a person to live to 200 years of age.

In studying the diet of these amazingly healthy old people, the Russians discovered that 70% of their caloric intake is of vegetable origin, particularly lettuce, cabbage, beans, spinach, corn, celery and parsley. Corn mush appears to be a part of every meal — eaten with a red pepper sauce. Fresh green vegetables are also a major part of every meal.

Two other areas of the world noted for longevity and an unusually high number of centenarians are Vilacamba in the Ecuadorian Andes, South America, and the Hunza region of Pakistan. In these two areas the importance of fresh vegetables is even more pronounced. In both regions meat and dairy products constitute a mere 1-1/2% of the total diet, the rest coming mostly from vegetables.

Other important factors for a long life, besides a vegetable-rich diet, are plenty of daily exercise (which you can get from gardening) and a pleasant disposition (which can also come from cultivating the soil).

Doctors recommend gardening for health reasons. So don't think of time spent in your garden as work — think of it as healthy exercise that will help you live longer and enjoy life.

Along with sleeping, eating is one of life's most important bodily functions. So, don't you think that the *quality* of the food you eat is deserving of a little consideration? Vegetables fresh from the garden not only have *better flavor* than store bought kinds (which generally have to be picked prematurely to ripen during transit) they are *nutritionally* superior. The longer you keep any vegetable, the greater the vitamin loss. You really can taste the difference. Try comparing sweet corn straight from the garden to one that has been left to stand just 12 hours after picking. Compare the flavor of a sun-ripened tomato to one that has been picked green and left to ripen indoors.

In fact, there are so many good reasons why you should cultivate a garden it's a wonder someone has not thought of passing a law guaranteeing land to everyone who wants to plant a garden. Perhaps someday they might.

Plant a Vegetable Garden
to Save $250

Addressing a meeting of the Future Farmers of America, in Kansas City, in October, 1974, President Ford made headlines with 12 ways to "Win" the fight against inflation. One of his recommendations was to "plant vegetable gardens."

To prove it can be done, the National Garden Bureau — headquartered near Gardenville, Pennsylvania — has designed a "Win" vegetable garden capable of feeding a family of four and saving more than $250.00 on food bills.

The garden size is 15 ft. wide by 25 ft. deep, and it features 19 varieties of vegetables capable of yielding a continuous supply of fresh vegetables from April through December, with plenty left over for canning, freezing and storing in a cool dry basement to provide food during non-gardening months.

First vegetables to be harvested in this garden are radish and spinach, which are sown early in spring as soon as the ground can be worked, followed by lettuce, beets, chard, peas and green onions.

Bush beans, broccoli, cucumbers, zucchini squash, cabbage, tomatoes, peppers, parsley and carrots continue the harvest through summer months, while cauliflower, Brussels sprouts, leeks — and second sowings of cabbage, lettuce, beets, radish, spinach and carrots — prolong the harvest through fall. In the case of spinach, leeks and Brussels sprouts crops can be harvested during winter months.

Vegetables representing some big savings are tomatoes and Brussels sprouts. When Brussels sprouts are grown as a fall and winter crop they mature at a time when store prices for fresh vegetables are high. They are frost hardy, and produce crops into December over most of the U.S.A.

Total value produced by the garden is $263.91 from which you have to deduct the costs of seed ($11.15). If the garden needs fertilizer, soil conditioner or pest controls these might add an additional $15.00 to the costs. The garden can be dug and managed by a spade, rake and trowel, which most homeowners already possess; and if a gardener prefers to have his plot rototilled ($15.00) or buy some of his vegetables as plants (say $10.00), savings of over $200 are still realistic. Labor can be written off as healthy exercise.

In addition to this financial saving, there are other benefits, including better-flavored vegetables and a higher nutritional value than anything you can buy in the store.

6

Yields	Savings
60 Cucumbers 25c each	$ 15.00
100 lbs. Tomatoes $1.00 for 3 lbs.	33.00
40 lbs. Zucchini 39c per lb.	15.60
20 lbs. Peppers 39c per lb.	7.80
24 heads Cabbage 39c head	9.36
48 heads Lettuce 49c head	23.52
30 lbs. Beans 39c lb.	11.10
48 lbs. Chard 59c lb.	28.32
36 lbs. Beets 29c lb.	10.44
50 lbs. Carrots 29c lb.	14.50
12 lbs. Spinach 59c lb.	7.08
24 bunches Radish 29c bunch	6.96
48 bunches Parsley 29c bunch	13.92
24 bunches Green Onions 25c bunch	6.00
28 bunches Leeks 58c bunch	16.52
24 heads Broccoli 49c head	11.76
12 heads Cauliflower 79c head	9.48
15 lbs. Peas 39c lb.	5.85
30 pts. Brussels Sprouts 59c pt.	17.70
TOTAL	$263.91

Seed Cost	
Cucumbers (Hybrid)	$ .75
Tomato (Hybrid)	.75
Zucchini Squash (Hybrid)	.75
Pepper (Hybrid)	.75
Cabbage	.35
Lettuce	.35
Bush Beans	.45
Carrots	.35
Chard	.50
Beets	.35
Spinach	.35
Radish	.35
Parsley	.35
Green Onion (Sets)	1.55
Leeks	.50
Broccoli (Hybrid)	.75
Cauliflower (Hybrid)	.75
Brussels Sprouts (Hybrid)	.75
Peas	.45
TOTAL	$11.15

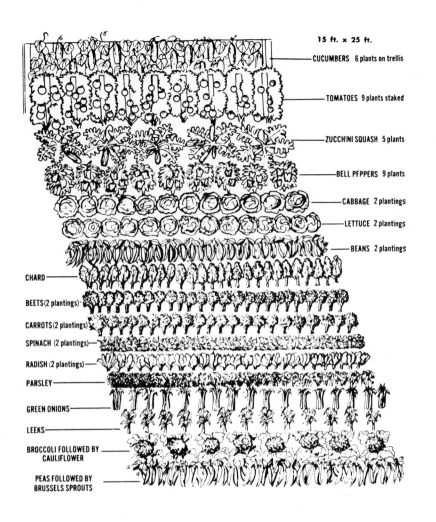

15 ft. x 25 ft.

— CUCUMBERS 6 plants on trellis

— TOMATOES 9 plants staked

— ZUCCHINI SQUASH 5 plants

— BELL PEPPERS 9 plants

— CABBAGE 2 plantings

— LETTUCE 2 plantings

— BEANS 2 plantings

CHARD

BEETS (2 plantings)

CARROTS (2 plantings)

SPINACH (2 plantings)

RADISH (2 plantings)

PARSLEY

GREEN ONIONS

LEEKS

BROCCOLI FOLLOWED BY CAULIFLOWER

PEAS FOLLOWED BY BRUSSELS SPROUTS

Vegetable Garden Plan

How to Use Vegetables From Your Garden

VEGETABLE	SALADS	COOKING	CANNING	FREEZING	STORING	OTHER REMARKS
Cucumbers	yes	—	yes	—	—	Especially good as pickles.
Tomatoes	yes	yes	yes	yes	—	Green tomatoes picked before frost will ripen indoors during winter.
Zucchini Squash	yes	yes	yes	yes		Can be used as substitute for cucumbers in salad.
Peppers	yes	yes	yes	yes	—	Especially good stuffed with meat.
Cabbage	yes	yes	yes	yes	—	Makes good sauerkraut for freezing.
Beans	yes	yes	yes	yes	yes	Dried beans store well for winter use.
Chard	yes	yes	—	yes	—	Very hardy. Lasts into winter months.
Beets	if cooked	yes	yes	yes	yes	Will store through winter in a box of moist sand in cool basement.
Carrots	yes	yes	yes	yes	yes	Will store through winter in a box of moist sand in cool basement.
Spinach	yes	yes	—	yes	—	Grows quickly during cool weather of spring and fall.
Radish	yes	yes	—	—	—	Can be braised to make a cooked vegetable.
Parsley	yes	—	—	yes	—	Used mostly as garnish.
Green Onions	yes	yes	yes	yes	—	Dried onions will keep during winter in a dry cool place.
Leeks	—	yes	—	yes	yes	Will keep during winter in a box of moist sand in cool basement.
Broccoli	—	yes	yes	yes	—	Plants grow one main head, and side shoots grow smaller heads.
Cauliflower	yes	yes	yes	yes	—	Best grown as a fall crop.
Peas	—	yes	yes	yes	—	Edible podded peas also good to grow.
Brussels Sprouts	—	yes	yes	yes	—	Best grown as a fall crop. Lasts well into winter.

Spacing

← 15 ft. →	
Cucumbers	2 ft.
Tomatoes	2 ft.
Zucchini Squash	2 ft.
Peppers	2 ft.
Cabbage	1½ ft.
Lettuce	1½ ft.
Beans	1½ ft.
Chard	1½ ft.
Beets	1 ft.
Carrots	1 ft.
Spinach	1 ft.
Radish	1 ft.
Parsley	1 ft.
Green Onions	1 ft.
Leeks	1 ft.
Broccoli/Cauliflower	2 ft.
Peas/Brussel Sprouts	2 ft.

25 ft.

Increase the Value of Your Garden

The "Win" vegetable garden featured here can be improved to gain greater productivity with just a few extra dollars of investment.

For example, the 15 ft. row of cucumbers can be planted for half of its length with cantaloupes, and as the fruits mature they can be supported with "slings" made from cloth or nylon stockings.

Instead of five hills of zucchini squash you can devote two to bush acorn squash.

Three pepper plants can be dropped to make room for eggplant.

The row of parsley can be cut down to a five foot row, and the remaining 10 ft. can be planted with turnips — one crop to mature in spring and the other in fall.

8

(Top) Golden zucchini squash is not only delicious and easy-to-grow, the novel fruits also are ornamental.

(Above) Carrots Chantenay Red Cored are a good all-purpose variety suitable for soils with a one-foot depth of loose soil.

(Top) Staked tomatoes occupy less space, keep fruit clean and are easier to pick. This variety is called "Delicious," growing some fruits that weigh up to 3 lbs. each.

(Center) Yellow Bermuda Onion has its roots in the soil and bulb above ground. The green spear-shaped stems have long since bent over and dried up indicating full maturity.

(Above) Lettuce Oakleaf is an excellent variety of looseleaf lettuce to start with, since it is heat resistant, and the more outer leaves you pick the more inner leaves will grow to take their place.

16 Easy Steps to Success

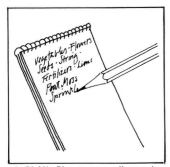

1. PLAN. Plan on paper the garden size and selection of varieties using the "WIN" garden as a model. Delete or substitute varieties according to personal preference and local conditions.

2. TEST. Test soil to determine acidity and need for lime.

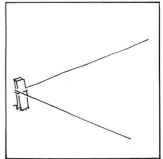

3. PROVIDE SUN. Select site in a sunny, well drained location. Start work on a dry day when soil is not wet or sticky.

4. STAKE. Stake out the area using string and pegs.

5. CONDITION SOIL. Apply soil conditioner such as peat moss or garden compost to the site if needed.

6. LIME. Sprinkle lime on acid soils at rate of 5 lbs. per 100 square feet every three years.

7. DIG. Dig over site to depth of 1 ft. Remove large stones and weed roots. Break up clods, mix in soil conditioner thoroughly.

8. FERTILIZE. Apply fertilizer at recommended rate.

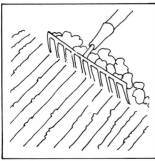

9. RAKE. Rake level. Remove small stones and weed roots.

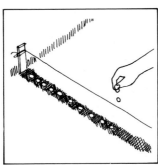

10. PLANT. Plant seeds or transplants, saving tender varieties until **after** last frost date.

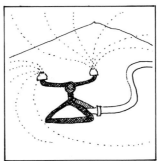

11. WATER. Water thoroughly at time of planting, also during dry spells. Even a week without drenching rain will reduce yields and slow down growth.

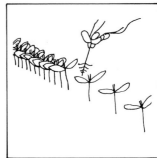

12. THIN. Thin seedlings, leaving room for strongest plants to develop fully.

13. WEED. Mulching helps control weeds. A few minutes a day is time better spent than trying to catch up on two weeks neglect.

14. CONTROL PESTS. Keep watch for pests and disease so early treatment can be administered. Check with local experienced gardeners to find out the main pest problems in your area and effective safe controls.

15. HARVEST. Pick fruit crops regularly. The more you pick the more will come.

16. SUCCESSION PLANT. Make succession plantings to gain maximum return from minimum space.

9

Planting & Care
for a Vegetable Garden

The three most important requirements for a successful vegetable garden are **moisture, sunlight** and **nutrients.** These three basic plant needs are more important to the production of plump succulent vegetables than to ornamentals such as flowers and house plants.

Moisture

The moisture for vegetables, however, must not be in the form of waterlogged soil. Good drainage throughout the season is essential and if the only spot in your yard is a waterlogged depression which cannot be drained, the easiest alternative is to create a raised bed of railroad ties or cinder blocks to a height of 1-1/2 feet on a bed of crushed stones.

Many times during a growing season there are dry spells, and even a week without a good soaking rain can stop or slow down the growth of most vegetables. The easiest way to ensure an adequate water supply is to set a common lawn sprinkler into the vegetable garden and let it soak the garden overnight.

Sunlight

At least six hours direct sunlight a day is needed for a productive vegetable garden. If shade falls on it at any time during the peak daylight hours it will slow down growth and reduce yields.

Borderline cases can be improved by using strips of aluminum kitchen foil between the rows as a mulch to increase the light intensity.

Plant Nutrients

There are more misconceptions about fertilizing a vegetable garden than any other activity. Many people believe that maintaining a compost site will add all the nutrients necessary. That just is not true. A compost pile can add nutrients *only* if it has been made from nutrient-bearing materials. A compost pile made largely from plant wastes and kitchen garbage will make a good soil conditioner when adequately decomposed, but its nutrient value is likely to be poor.

For a compost pile to add nutrients to the soil it must be made properly — built-up like a layer cake, enclosed on all sides to prevent leaking and thoroughly turned over at intervals to speed decomposition and ensure a good mixture of the ingredients. Also, it's better to have two piles side by side — one that has already decomposed for adding to the garden, and one that is being built.

An easier way to add nutrients is to buy a commercial fertilizer in package form, which has the major ingredients mixed in the right balance. There is no difference between phosphorus you buy in a package and phosphorus that comes from a compost pile. Phosphorus is phosphorus, just as Vitamin C is Vitamin C whether you take it as a pill or in the form of an orange.

The only difference is that compost properly made adds both nutrients and conditions the soil, while the packaged fertilizer adds nutrients pure and simple.

The three major plant nutrients are nitrogen, phosphorous and potash, and the proportion of these in any given fertilizer is shown as percentages such as 5-10-5 or 28-26-10.

Packaged fertilizer is available in different forms. It can be in granular form for sprinkling onto the soil and raking into the upper surface; it can be in concentrated liquid form for mixing with water and spraying onto plants. This last method is known as foliar feeding because the nutrients are taken up by the plant through its leaves rather than its roots.

The easiest most convenient fertilizer is the granular type that needs no mixing or spray equipment — you just sprinkle it on the soil before planting at the recommended rate.

However, there are two kinds of fertilizer in this group — fast release and slow release. Fast release fertilizer will carry a warning that the fertilizer should be applied at least 10 days *before* planting, otherwise the concentrated nitrogen can induce injury to plants, called "burning". Slow release fertilizer is the better buy. It is formulated so that the nitrogen is released in small regular amounts over long periods — just enough to get young seedlings off to a good start, and then in regular amounts to keep plants growing well throughout the season. The slow release fertilizer can be applied at planting time without risk of burning.

Another disadvantage with fast release fertilizer is that booster applications must be made during the growing season — particularly with fruiting vegetables such as tomatoes and peppers. With slow release fertilizer one application is generally enough.

An over-supply of nitrogen in the soil can be detrimental to fruiting crops because it causes too much leaf growth, and not enough fruit formation. In tomatoes, a disease called blossom end rot is also caused by too much nitrogen. This is why an over-abundance of animal manure (rich in nitrogen) can slow down fruit ripening and induce blossom-end rot. Soils high in animal manures *must* be compensated with high phosphorous levels in order to encourage early fruit formation and ripening.

Soil Preparation

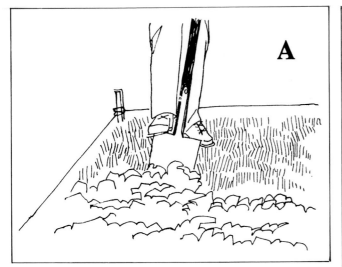

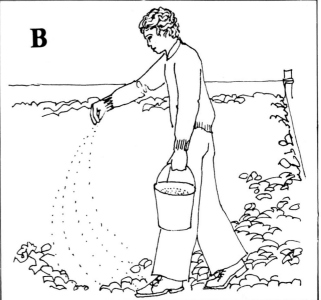

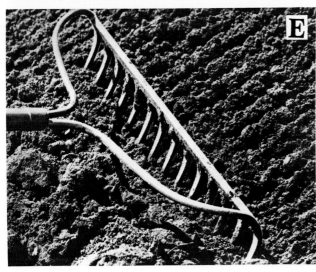

A. Mark out the site with string and dig over to a depth of 1 ft., removing stones and weed roots. Work in soil conditioner at same time if needed.

B. Add fertilizer. In acid soil areas also add lime at the rate of 5 lbs. per 100 sq. feet every three years.

C. Rake fertilizer into the upper soil surface. Remove smaller stones and weed roots.

D & E. Finish up with a finely raked, level site ready for planting

How to Build a Compost Pile

Before you start to make a compost pile you must first decide what you want from it. Do you want it basically as a soil conditioner to improve the texture of a sandy or clay soil, relying on commercial fertilizer for nutrients, or do you want it to serve both as a soil conditioner *and* an all inclusive fertilizer?

As a soil conditioner only, your compost pile is very easy to make. You can simply pile all kinds of kitchen wastes, grass clippings and shredded leaves into a corner and allow it to decompose into a fine crumbly dark soil. No garden should be without this kind of compost pile. Vegetable gardens *always* need organic soil conditioners. The action of wind, sun and heavy footsteps leads to soil compaction which in turn is improved by adding garden compost, and helps commercial fertilizer do its job properly.

In the Organic Gardening Encyclopedia there are 10 pages devoted to composting. It is not a haphazard project.

If you want a compost pile that serves *both* as a soil conditioner and all inclusive fertilizer, then the procedure is completely different. Here's what you must do:

1 — Choose a level site and enclose it in on all four sides.

2 — Build the pile up like a layer cake, starting off with a six inch layer of *plant material,* such as straw, leaves, sawdust and kitchen wastes.

3 — Then a two inch layer of animal manure.

4 — Then a 1/4 inch of top-soil.

5 — On top of this add a vegetable fertilizer containing the three essential plant nutrients — nitrogen, phosphorus and potash. Alternatively, add organic materials containing these nutrients (see list at end of this chapter).

6 — This sandwich is then watered and the process repeated until the heap is several feet high.

The heap should be made loosely to aid ventilation, and not matted down. Tremendous heat will be generated in the middle, and the pile will shrink as micro-organisms activate the decomposition process.

After several weeks the heap should be turned with a pitch-fork, placing the outside inside. After a period of three months the heap should be sufficiently decomposed to use on the garden. Use at any time, but especially in winter or at time of digging the soil prior to transplanting. Side-dressings between rows are also beneficial.

Actually, there are many different composting systems, and the one above is given as an example because it is the easiest. The following materials can also be added to the pile in order to improve its nutrient content, although they are not necessary if you use a commercial fertilizer containing the three essential plant nutrients.

12

Nitrogen (N) needed for healthy green leaves	Dried Blood Cottonseed Meal Fish Scrap Activated Sludge Vegetable Residue Hot Manure (rabbit hen, sheep, horse) Peanut Shells
Phosphorus (P) needed to help fruit reach maturity	Rock Phosphate Basic Slag Bone Meal Dried Blood
Potash (K) for good root and kernel development; also helps fight soil disease and this element improves the keeping quality of fruit	Greensand Granite Dust Wood Ashes Cold Manure (cow) Seaweed, Kelp Cocoa Shells Plant Residues

Soil Care

Good soil is the foundation of a successful vegetable garden, and "tilth" is the term used by farmers to describe the physical make-up of soil in which vegetable crops thrive. Soil with "good tilth" is loose and crumbly to a depth of at least 1 ft. before hitting shale or clay clods, and one that is free of debris and rocks.

Clay and sandy soils have poor tilth. Clay soils are too heavy, cold and prone to waterlogging in wet weather or baking hard as a rock in dry weather. Plant roots cannot penetrate freely to absorb soil nutrients, and to improve a clay soil it is necessary to dig up and mix in liberal quantities of soil conditioner such as peat moss, leaf mold, decomposed animal manures and garden compost.

At the other extreme are sandy soils, which have no moisture holding capacity and allow plant nutrients to escape too rapidly. Sandy soils are also improved by addition of soil conditioners to add substance and body.

The actions of wind, sun and heavy footsteps on a garden lead to compaction of the soil, so it is always wise to keep adding soil conditioner — especially in the form of garden compost, peat moss or animal manures when available.

Animal Manure

With the widespread disappearance of farmyard animals gardeners have had to rely more and more on commercial fertilizers.

In England, when a horse passes down the street and leaves a few droppings in the road, immediately you will see a hoard of Englishmen rush out with buckets and shovels, converge on the steaming pile and fight over who gets it. England — a nation of expert gardeners — knows the value of horse manure.

I have never kept a horse, yet I have never had any trouble locating good manure. Towns and cities are surrounded by suburbs and country where horses and other manure producing animals can be found within easy driving distance. Manure can be bought by the bag-load, trunk load — or delivered right to your door in a dump truck. Or, with a little ingenuity, you can find a friendly stable willing to have you haul away as much as you please. A horse produces 18,000 lbs. of the good stuff annually, and it can provide a disposal problem for some horse owners.

What I do is to save supermarket bags, especially the double-lined kind. Then I fill the bags neatly and cleanly with well-decomposed manure and haul it away, eight bags at a time in my car trunk — 24 if you have a station wagon. Well decomposed manure is the key. You can tell just by looking and feeling it. Fresh manure tends to be soggy, soft, heavy and it stinks. Well decomposed manure is dark, crumbly and feels so clean you could sleep in it.

Well-decomposed manure can be added to your garden at any time, as a mulch in spring or as a side-dressing in summer to help plants along. But fall is the best time for a heavy application, and for a newly dug garden that may mean spreading it to a depth of 4 inches, leaving it there over winter, and digging it into the soil in spring before seeding.

In my experience well-decomposed manure works wonders on leaf crops like cabbage, lettuce, chard and broccoli, and does miracles with onions, but with fruiting crops like tomatoes, peppers and melons it tends to create too much leaf growth, and poor fruit production or late ripening because of the high nitrogen. For this reason it is always a wise precaution to use plenty of bonemeal (a source of phosphorus) or a commercial fertilizer high in phosphorus to speed up fruit development.

Soil Testing

A soil test to determine the acidity of your soil is a good policy.

Acid soils benefit from a dressing of lime every three years at the rate of 5 lbs. per 100 sq. ft., and if you don't know what kind of soil you have check around with local gardeners to determine whether your soil is acid. If in doubt, a soil test will tell you. This can be done by sending a sample from several parts of your garden to the local state university or a commercial testing service. Garden centers also sell soil-testing kits.

Fortunately, vegetables tolerate a wide range of soil conditions. Most vegetables favor a slightly acid to neutral soil. Alkaline soils are found in limestone regions, salt marshes and desert areas. Use of manure and compost as soil conditioners will help to improve an alkaline soil.

The need for soil tests is greatly exaggerated in my opinion. If one vegetable prefers a certain range and another prefers something else, how can you possibly create ideal conditions from one row to the next? Impossible! Use of lime in an acid soil will help you strike that happy medium.

Good soil practices, like the use of soil conditioners, will keep the soil in good heart.

Weed Control

Regular hoeing between crops during the growing season keeps down weeds and helps roots breathe to produce better results. A garden smothered in weeds cannot produce worthwhile results, and a few minutes weeding each day before the sun goes down is better than trying to catch up on two weeks neglect.

Mulching

The advantages of mulching a vegetable garden far outweigh the disadvantages. Against mulching is the school of thought that says mulch attracts mice, slugs and other pests. On the other hand, mulching keeps down weeds, conserves soil moisture, maintains an even soil temperature, and helps to keep fruit crops like tomatoes and peppers clean.

There are many kinds of materials that can be used as mulch, and in spite of many tests throughout the country there is wide disagreement on the most effective. Like many aspects of vegetable gardening it depends on your soil, your location, the kinds of crops you grow and a dozen other variables. Some universal favorites, however, are the following:

Straw. Crisp, clean, brown straw in my opinion is the best mulching material. It looks good, is easy to obtain, and is inexpensive. A light six inch layer between rows of vegetables will smother most weeds, and the occasional few that do break through are easily pulled by hand.

Other organic materials that will work in a similar way to straw are shredded leaves, grass clippings, pine needles, chopped bark, newspapers (ugly), cocoa bean hulls, corn cobs and similar fibrous materials that will eventually break down, decompose and become a useful part of the soil.

Plastic. Black plastic has proven to be especially beneficial to warm weather crops such as tomatoes, peppers, eggplant, pumpkins, squash and melons. The black color helps to absorb heat and maintains a high soil temperature when nights get cold.

The black plastic is laid down in strips at time of planting and holes are cut at the required row distances for transplants to be set in place. Edges of the plastic are then covered with soil to prevent wind from ripping it up.

Seed Starting & Transplanting

Certain varieties of vegetables are best planted from seeds sown directly into the garden. These include all root crops such as carrots and radishes, plus peas, beans and corn.

Other vegetables are best started early indoors or else purchased as healthy transplants from a garden center or nursery specializing in bedding plants.

Choose Healthy Transplants

Young plants are more susceptible to harm in the first seven days after transplanting into the garden than at any other time of their development. Tender plants such as tomatoes, peppers, eggplants and cucumbers should not be planted until all danger of frost is past, since planting too early is probably the biggest cause of loss among these vegetables.

Just as there are good and poor quality seeds, it's possible to have good and poor quality transplants. Here are some ways to recognize a top quality transplant :

1 — Avoid long, lanky specimens that have had to stretch towards the light, or have produced a spindly growth owing to overcrowding of roots. A dwarf, compact, sturdy plant is better than a tall, thin, straggly specimen.

2 — Look for healthy dark green color in tomatoes, peppers and most other popular vegetable plants. Plants with shrivelled leaves, yellow leaves or wilted leaves should be avoided.

3 — When you buy plants in peat pots gently tear off the bottom of the pot and release the roots. Although roots will penetrate through the peat, and the peat eventually decomposes, a dry period could keep roots pot-bound and hinder good development. To ensure a healthy plant gently remove the bottom or sides without tearing roots.

Immediately after transplanting water all plants thoroughly.

Following are some of the easiest ways to start seeds yourself with the object of growing good size plants for setting out into the garden when conditions are favorable.

Peat Pots

Peat pots like those shown are a good way to start many types of seeds. The pots are filled with a planting soil, then several seeds sown on top and covered over. After the seeds have sprouted the smaller seedlings can be thinned out to leave one sturdy, healthy plant to occupy the entire pot. The peat sides are porous and the roots will penetrate right through. Although these peat walls will decompose in the soil, given adequate moisture, it is a good policy at transplanting time to peel away the bottom of each pot to allow more freedom for the roots to grow deep into the soil. They are also available in kit form with planting soil from catalog houses and stores.

Peat Pellets

Peat pellets are another easy way to grow both large and small seeded varieties of flowers and vegetables. When water is added to the pellet it immediately swells to seven times its original height. The soft moist peat then makes an ideal growing medium for many kinds of plants. At transplanting time the netting around the peat is easily removed to allow the roots complete freedom to grow. Tomatoes, peppers, cauliflowers, broccoli and cabbage are especially good vegetables to start in peat pellets. They are available in kit form with plastic watering trays to hold the pellets. A new type of peat pellet without a net is also available.

Peat & Plastic Planters

Peat or plastic planters are good to start fine seeds, such as asparagus and lettuce. The usual method is to fill the planters with a pre-packaged soil mix, make several lines of furrows with a flat edge, and sow the seed thinly along the furrows. Keep moist with a fine spray, and transfer the seedlings to individual positions when they have developed a true set of leaves.

Seed Tapes

Seed tapes save time in spacing certain small-seeded vegetables, and planting them is easy either indoors in a seed flat or directly into the garden. First you dig a shallow furrow to the recommended depth, stretch the tape along the furrow, cover with fine soil and water lightly each day until seeds sprout. The seeds are pre-spaced in the tape, which is soluble and disappears quickly once it is in the ground, leaving the seeds free to germinate. Try radish, carrots, lettuce and beets. Seed tapes are readily available both from mail order seed catalogs and local stores.

Pre-Planters

Most stores during spring will sell pre-planted packs of popular flower and vegetable seeds. These packs generally consist of a plastic container filled with planting soil, and seeds pre-spaced for reliable germination. All that is needed to start growing is to strip away the clear film cover and add water. The packs are deep enough to allow plants to reach a good size before transplanting, and they fit easily on a windowsill. After transplanting, the empty plastic pack makes a fine container to grow parsley or cress. Parsley will need soil and a sunny location, but for cress all you need is some absorbent paper tissue as a liner, and the cress will grow in it happily even in a shaded window.

14

(Above) Tomato seedlings growing in Jiffy-7 peat pellets on a kitchen windowsill. A netting around the peat can be gently removed at time of transplanting to give roots complete freedom to spread.

(Top, left) Lettuce seedlings growing in a peat planter. Although they appear crowded, these young seedlings are the right size for transplanting outdoors, and can be easily separated at this stage.

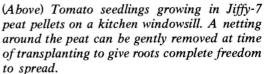

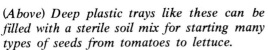

(Above) Deep plastic trays like these can be filled with a sterile soil mix for starting many types of seeds from tomatoes to lettuce.

(Center, left) Peat pots like these — either square-shaped or round — are good for starting tomatoes, peppers and eggplants.

(Center, right) This pre-planter has a clear plastic lid punched with holes. Seeds are already set into the soil mix, and once water is poured through the holes the seeds will germinate. All you add is water.

(Right) Seed tapes unravel to form a straight row, with seeds pre-spaced to save thinning.

Hardening Off

There is a real temptation to plant early and get a jump on your neighbors by having the first peas or the first tomatoes, and unfortunately planting too early is the biggest cause of plant losses.

Many seed packets say, "plant as soon as the soil can be worked," particularly on hardy varieties, like peas, beets, lettuce, radish, carrots and spinach. But that is misleading. Certainly these varieties will tolerate mild frosts, but they *will not germinate* until the soil is sufficiently warm. So your seeds will just sit there and do nothing until the temperature rises. In the meantime you are likely to get impatient, slander the seeds as being no good, and replant. You can actually feel if the soil is cold.

For warm weather crops it is essential to wait until after the last frost date before planting out, and even then your plants should be hardened off if they have been started indoors. The "shock" of transplanting any vegetable from an indoor environment to the outdoors can be so great that the plants never really recover.

When you buy plants from garden centers ask if they have been hardened-off. If not it's easy to make a "cold frame" which will do the job. Cold frames can be purchased ready made, but it's easy to throw one together without much expense. A wooden box sunk into the soil and a sheet of glass over it is often adequate for small gardens. Simply set the young plants in it, and cover with the glass at night. After a week of this treatment they will be ready to face the outside world.

(Above) For large vegetable gardens professional cold frames like this can be purchased — made from wood or aluminum. For small gardens this expense is unnecessary...

(Below) For small gardens where you need to harden off a few tomato, pepper and cabbage plants, all you need is a wooden box sunk into the ground and covered with glass at night.

16

COOL SEASON CROPS
(Can Be Planted Four Weeks Before Last Frost Date)

Beets	Leeks
★ Broccoli	Onions
★ Brussels Sprouts	★ Parsley
★ Cabbage	Parsnips
Carrots	Potato (Irish)
★ Cauliflower	Radish
Celery	Rhubarb (seeds or roots)
Chard	Salsify
Kale	Spinach
Kohlrabi	Turnips

WARM SEASON CROPS
(Plant After Last Frost Date)

Beans, Snap	★ Pepper
Beans, Lima	Pumpkin
Cantaloupe	Squash
Corn	Sunflower
Cucumber	Sweet Potato
★ Eggplant	★ Tomato
Okra	Watermelon
Peanuts	

★ These can be bought as transplants from garden centers, or seed can be started six to eight weeks earlier indoors to grow your own healthy transplants.

AVERAGE PLANTING DATES

Location	Cool Season Crops	Warm Season Crops
New York	April 15	May 15
Chicago	April 15	May 15
Detroit	April 15	May 15
Philadelphia	April 15	May 15
Cleveland	April 15	May 15
Boston	April 15	May 15
Washington DC	April 15	May 15
Los Angeles	November 15	March 15
Denver	May 1	June 1
Hartford	April 15	May 15
Minneapolis	April 15	May 15
Milwaukee	April 15	May 15
Pittsburgh	April 15	May 15
San Francisco	October 15	March 15
Omaha	April 15	May 15
Columbus	April 15	May 15
Seattle	April 15	May 15
St Louis	April 15	May 15
Cincinnati	April 15	May 15
Baltimore	April 15	May 15
Dayton	April 15	May 15
Harrisburg	April 15	May 15
Providence	April 15	May 15
Kansas City	April 15	May 15
Wichita	April 15	May 15
Indianapolis	April 15	May 15
Tampa	November 1	January 1
Buffalo	May 1	June 1
Atlanta	March 15	April 15
Dallas	November 1	March 15
Memphis	April 15	May 15

Planting & Transplanting

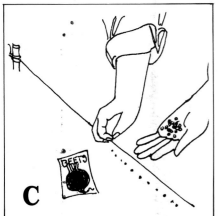

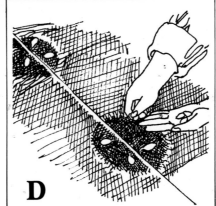

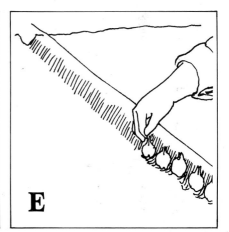

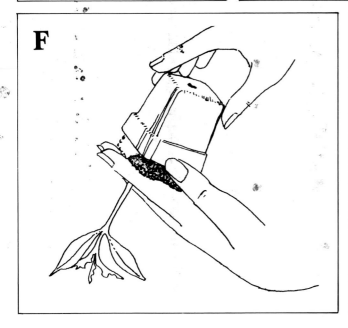

A. Mark planting rows with string. For small seeds make furrow with end of hoe handle.

B. For larger seeds and onion sets make deeper furrow with hoe blade, or a trowel.

C. Sow small seeds evenly to make thinning easier.

D. Cucumber and squash can be planted in "hills" or groups, with three or four seeds planted to each group.

E. When planting onion sets, they can be spaced close together, and thinned by harvesting as "scallions," leaving some to mature into full-size onions.

F. To remove transplants from pots slide a knife around the edge, grip the base of the stem between two fingers, turn upside down, and slide the plant out with root system intact.

17

Planting Perennial Vegetables

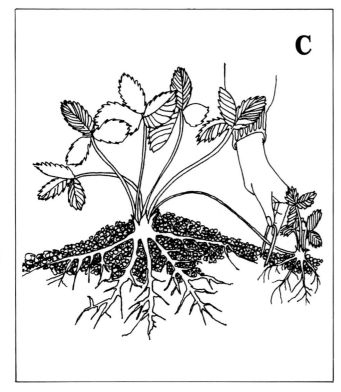

Asparagus, rhubarb and strawberries are examples of vegetables and fruits which are perennial — coming up year after year without replanting. These plants should always be kept together in a special area of your garden. Feed each year with a vegetable garden fertilizer in spring and fall to keep plants established and healthy.

A. Asparagus roots need planting in trenches 8-12 inches deep enriched with good garden compost and vegetable fertilizer. Do not fill in the trench all at one time. Cover crowns with four inches of soil and as the shoots grow, fill up the trench to ground level. Figure on 12-15 roots per adult.

B. Two rhubarb plants are plenty for a family of four. Dig separate holes one foot deep, and enrich the bottom six inches with good garden compost and vegetable fertilizer. Rest roots on top of this and cover with three inches of soil. As shoots sprout fill in rest of hole to ground level.

C. After several years a strawberry bed will need replanting with young, healthy stock. This is best done by buying new virus-free plants, but if you like you can create your own by pegging a runner into the soil or into a pot. During fruit-bearing years runners are best removed so all energy is directed into flower and fruit formation.

Staking to Save Space

A

B

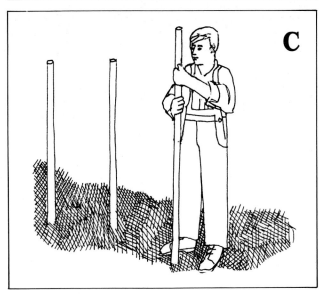

C

D

Tomato vines left to sprawl on the ground occupy more space, but generally will produce heavier yields.

A. To save space cucumbers can be encouraged to climb. Durable netting made of plastic cord is best, supported by stout poles and hung from steel wire.

B. Garden netting like this can be used to support pole beans, peas, malabar spinach, and melons in addition to cucumbers.

C. To support tomato plants sink stakes into the ground. To deter wood boring pests, coat the stake below ground with a wood preservative.

D. Staking tomatoes like this is highly recommended for small gardens. They can be planted closer together this way, the fruit is easier to pick, it stays clean, and reduces the chance of sunscald. Also, staking looks neater, and neatness counts a lot in vegetable gardens.

Plant Hardiness Map

Planting guides such as plant hardiness maps are supposed to tell you two things —
a. the last expected frost date of spring and the first expected frost date of fall. From these dates you are supposed to be able to determine the length of growing season in your area for tender plants.
b. the average minimum winter temperatures for each zone as a guide to winter hardiness of tender plants.

Unfortunately, even the best zone maps can do more harm than good unless you seek a second opinion from a local authority. For example, many official plant zone maps show that my area of Pennsylvania has a last frost date of April 20th. However, I can assure you that in the past eight years I have lived in the area there has been only *one* year when that was true. All other years killing frosts have been closer to May 10th, and even later.

Also, there are many regions of the country with micro-climates — areas too small to show on a normal map, and I know of many friends who brag about being able to grow plants successfully that are not recommended for their area.

When in doubt about frost dates and adaptability of plants for your area *don't rely entirely on a Plant Hardiness Map* — check locally among more experienced gardening friends, or with a local reputable nursery, extension service agent or botanical garden.

Gardening in the Shade

A vegetable garden needs at least 6 hours direct sunlight each day in order to be productive. If you live among trees which cast heavy shadows during summer months you cannot expect to grow vegetables. It's true there are shade-loving flowers such as begonias and impatiens, but with vegetables there is no such luck — with the exception of mushrooms, garden cress and bean sprouts — which are best grown in containers indoors (see chapter on container gardening).

There is one trick, however, which can improve your chances of growing vegetables in a shaded area. Simply use rolls of aluminum foil as a mulch. The aluminum foil will act as a light reflector increasing the amount of light around your plants. It will certainly improve your chances of growing easy crops such as bush beans and lettuce.

Even gardens that do receive good sunlight sometimes have a corner that gets shaded early in the day — by the shadow of a tall tree or the corner of a house. This happens to my own garden, and tomato plants at one end used to grow too slowly — until I hit upon the idea of using the aluminum foil. This increased their share of light so they kept pace with other tomato plants in the sunniest part of the garden.

University experiment stations have even used aluminum foil as a mulch for tomatoes that receive ample sunlight, and they have found that the foil reflector will increase yields and improve earliness.

Succession Planting

To gain maximum value from a vegetable garden succession planting is essential. By succession planting we mean gaining two plantings to each garden row — one to mature in summer, the other in fall.

For example, spinach is an early crop — it requires sowing as early in the spring as possible, so it matures before hot weather sets in. This will leave a space for another planting later in the summer to mature in fall when cooler weather returns.

Peas are another crop that bear early and are finished by early summer. That same space can then be dug over and re-planted with another row of broccoli, cauliflower or Brussels sprouts to mature during fall of the same year.

Corn reaches a peak in mid-summer, and the space it occupies can be replanted with a fall crop of cabbage, lettuce, or broccoli.

The following are some varieties of vegetables which can be double-cropped by a planting in spring followed by another in mid-summer for fall harvesting:

Lettuce, beets, carrots, spinach, turnips, bush beans, broccoli, cauliflower, cabbage and radish.

Certain vegetable varieties do better as a fall crop than a spring or summer crop. These include broccoli, cauliflower and Brussels sprouts. They prefer to be planted in mid-summer so they mature during the cool weather of fall. Brussels sprouts planted this way are especially valuable, since the green sprouts can be picked into December over most of the United States when store prices for green vegetables are high.

Other vegetables take a long growing season to mature properly. These include leeks, pumpkins, winter squash, salsify and parsnips, so double cropping with these is not possible.

The best group of vegetables to grow in a home vegetable garden are those which mature reasonably early and stay productive over the entire gardening season, surviving a wide range of conditions. These super-productive vegetables are zucchini squash, chard, parsley, tomatoes and peppers.

Question: I was very happy with the sweet corn that I grew last year, so I saved the seed to plant this year, but the results were disappointing in spite of the same care and attention.

Answer: It doesn't pay to save seed from year to year either from left-over seed packets or from seed saved from plants. Many vegetables — sweet corn in particular — are hybrids which produce vigorous growth and abundant yields the first season. However, since they are the result of complicated cross-breeding the benefits are lost in the second generation, resulting in poor growth and reduced yields.

Planting & Harvesting Chart

The following planting and harvesting times are approximate, and will vary according to location. In areas of the South and Southern California planting and harvesting times are earlier. For a better guide to planting dates, refer to the table on page 16 showing average planting dates for major cities in the United States.

Days to maturity shown after each vegetable variety are for optimum growing conditions where adequate sunlight, moisture and nutrients can ensure steady, continuous growth. Daytime and night-time temperatures also have an effect on growing conditions.

VARIETY	Feb.	Mar.	Apr.	May.	June.	July.	Aug.	Sept.	Oct.	Nov.	Dec.
Beans, Snap (50-60 days)											
Beets (55-60 days)											
Broccoli (60-80 days)											
Brussels Sprouts (90-100 days) *											
Cabbage (70-80 days) *											
Cantaloupe (80-90 days)											
Carrots (70-80 days)											
Cauliflower (60-80 days) *											
Celery (120-140 days)											
Corn (80-90 days)											
Cucumbers (60-70 days)											
Eggplant (70-80 days) *											
Leeks (130-140 days)											
Lima Beans (75-90 days)											
Looseleaf Lettuce (50-60 days)											
Okra (60-70 days)											
Onions (100-120 days)											
Parsley (80-90 days)											
Parsnips (100-120 days)											
Peas (65-70 days)											
Peppers (70-80 days) *											
Pumpkin (100-120 days)											
Radish (25-30 days)											
Spinach (50-60 days)											
Squash, Summer (55-65 days)											
Squash, Winter (90-110 days)											
Swiss Chard (60-70 days)											
Tomatoes (70-80 days) *											
Turnips (45-60 days)											
Watermelon (75-90 days)											
* Days from transplanting											

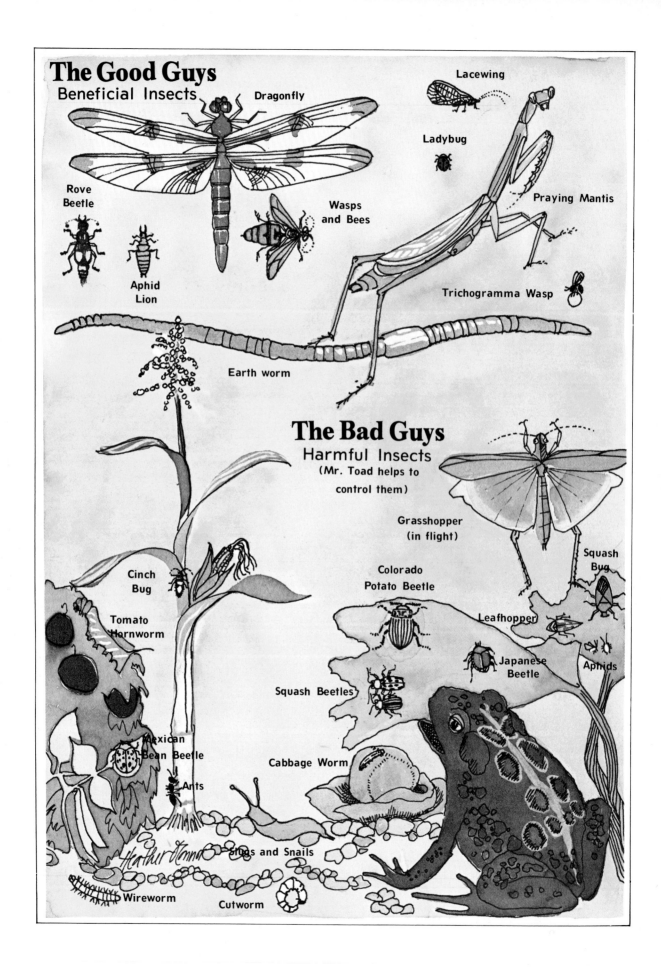

The Good Guys
Beneficial Insects

Dragonfly

Lacewing

Ladybug

Praying Mantis

Rove Beetle

Wasps and Bees

Aphid Lion

Trichogramma Wasp

Earth worm

The Bad Guys
Harmful Insects
(Mr. Toad helps to control them)

Grasshopper (in flight)

Squash Bug

Cinch Bug

Colorado Potato Beetle

Leafhopper

Tomato Hornworm

Japanese Beetle

Aphids

Squash Beetles

Mexican Bean Beetle

Cabbage Worm

Ants

Wireworm

Slugs and Snails

Cutworm

22

Pest Control

There is a great deal of controversy about "organic" and "inorganic" principles of gardening, as well as a great deal of misunderstanding about what constitutes an organic gardener.

For example, it is wrong to think that every garden aid that comes out of a package is a hazard to the environment. There are many manufactured pest controls developed from organic compounds, and it is ridiculous not to consider using commercial controls when pests reach plague proportions, and threaten complete destruction of the garden.

That has happened to me in the case of slugs. Frogs and dishes of stale beer are the prescribed "organic" remedies for dealing with slugs, but in spite of a pond full of frogs and gallons of stale beer, slugs continued to strip every edible leaf in the garden — even marigold plants which were the first to fall victim. In desperation I bought a package of slug pellets, and was very happy with the results. Instead of no garden I had a beautiful garden, and I have the slug pellets to thank for it.

On the other hand, I find wood ashes to be an effective vegetable dust, and a bucketful will go a long way to protecting seedlings from insects and rabbits. Pest controls made from pyrethrum (an African plant) and diatomaceous dust are also effective against chewing insects, and organically approved.

If you are a beginner you won't know what disease and insect pests are prevalent in your area until you've been through a growing season, and gained first-hand experience, so pest control the first year will largely consist of keeping a watchful eye for first signs of trouble, and dealing with it before it gets out of hand. Local nurseries and garden centers are generally the best places to go for advice.

Another good policy if your garden is new is to seek advice from neighbors, relatives and friends close-by, who are already gardeners. They will know the most troublesome pests, and can tell you how they deal with them.

Where dogs, cats and rabbits pose a problem I have found that a two-foot high chicken-wire fence all around the garden works wonders. It's cheap to buy in rolls, is easy to set in place, and provides adequate protection from the majority of wandering animals.

For organic enthusiasts the following controls may prove of some benefit:

Praying Mantis — eats many harmful insects smaller than itself.

Marigolds — discourages nematodes (microscopic worms that invade root systems) and is repellent to rabbits. Slugs and Japanese beetles relish marigolds, however.

Wood Ashes — effective as a vegetable dust to deter chewing pests. Needs applying after every rain to be fully effective.

Ladybugs — for control of aphids, mites, thrips, budworms, bollworms.

Trichogramma Wasps — kill bagworms, cabbage maggots, fruit tree pests.

Milky Spore — controls Japanese beetles.

Bacillus Thuringiensis — controls inchworms and caterpillars.

Stale beer — drowns slugs, but not effective in plague proportions.

Birds — many birds, especially robins, are beneficial in catching all kinds of insect pests, particularly cut worms and Japanese beetles. Consider birds a friend of the garden and not an enemy. Pheasant and crows can do great damage to newly sprouted seedlings, and a string with flashing discs will act as a good scaring device when plants are vulnerable.

Frogs — control slugs and many other harmful grubs.

Cats — deter rabbits, control destructive moles, shrews and mice.

Earthworms — condition the soil.

Alternatively, you can save yourself a lot of trouble by checking with your local garden supply center for a safe, easy-to-use pest control, many of which are formulated to deal with a wide range of pest problems. Because of bans on *DDT* and concern over other hazardous chemicals, manufacturers are being much more cautious in the manufacture of pest controls, giving increasing attention to the question of environmental safety.

23

Essential Equipment

Most gardeners make the mistake of over-spending on equipment when they begin. For small gardens under 15 ft. by 25 ft. in size it is easy enough to get by with a spade for digging, a rake for leveling the site and creating a fine soil surface, a trowel for planting and a hoe for weeding. In 15 years of gardening I have used little else.

Machine cultivators are expensive, and rental of this kind of equipment is better than outright purchase of up to $500.00 unless you are cultivating a 1/4 acre or more, and intend to sell produce from a farm stand to recover the investment quickly.

Here are the more common kinds of tools necessary for good gardening. Most gardeners will find they need little else.

Wheelbarrow. Indispensable for carting off weed roots and rocks, moving compost, carting tools and dozens of other land-carrying uses.

Spade for digging and breaking up the soil.

Fork for handling mulch, animal manures, lifting potatoes, breaking up soil.

Rake for finer soil surface work such as leveling and catching weed roots and stones. Top end of rake can be used to make furrows for seeds.

Trowel and Hand Fork can be used for planting and removing weeds.

Dandelion Weeder can be used for removing deep rooted weeds, and is handy to make furrows for seeds. Also useful as an asparagus knife to cut asparagus at soil.

Hoe is necessary for loosening soil, to keep it from compacting and for removing weeds. Edge of hoe also helps to make seed furrows.

Sieve is a good tool to have where soil is choked with stones and weed roots. Soil piled into sieve will fall through as fine granules, trapping clay particles and trash.

Sprayer for applying liquid fertilizer and pest control. The model shown will adequately spray even tall fruit trees. For a simple vegetable garden and dwarf fruit trees an inexpensive hand-held plastic sprayer is adequate.

Bucket for holding lime, supplies, hauling water.

Watering Can for irrigation. Alternatively, use garden hose and sprinkler for watering.

24

Small Gardens Pay Big

Even if you have never gardened in your life before you can succeed beyond your wildest dreams in growing flavorful, vitamin-rich fresh vegetables by keeping your garden small, and growing varieties that give maximum yields from minimum work and minimum expense.

Small gardens are less work, more fun and greatly rewarding — providing you follow a few simple common sense rules. The formula for success is neither a large yard, nor a mass of expensive equipment. Success depends on *keeping things simple.*

Pictured above is a *single plant* of a wax bush bean called *Brittle Wax.* This engraving — which appeared in a 1903 seed catalog — is a faithful reproduction of an actual plant which yielded 87 pods. The record for one plant, however, is 167 pods, grown by a Canadian vegetable gardener.

Brittle Wax is still a popular variety sold in seed catalogs today, but in the space of 70 years there have been numerous improvements to wax beans in terms of yield, pod size, flavor and disease resistance.

This kind of productivity is far easier to achieve in a small vegetable garden than a large one, where a person can devote proper attention to soil cultivation. weeding and pest control.

The larger the area you try to cultivate, the more demanding it is of your time, and the less successful you will be in growing crops like this.

What's more, when you cultivate a small area carefully you can space vegetables much closer together than the text books advise. At Michigan State University I have seen dwarf peach trees and apples growing in *12 in. clay pots* yielding regular-size fruit, and lettuce planted shoulder-to-shoulder in broad rows rather than single straight lines.

Leopold Klein, of Valley Stream, New York, wrote to me shortly after an article I wrote appeared in the Long Island Press. He enclosed a picture of four tomato plants growing in an area just 2 ft. by 2 ft., from which he harvested *100 lbs.* of tomatoes.

It doesn't take much for nature to yield her bountiful harvests!

Mr. Klein's most successful system involves growing four tomato plants in a wooden box measuring 24 inches by 24 inches by 20 inches deep, filled with a soil mixture of equal parts garden soil, sand and peat moss enriched with fertilizer containing nitrogen, phosphorus and potassium.

Healthy foot-high transplants grown indoors in

empty milk cartons and hardened off outside under plastic tents are set into the box spaced one to each side at a distance of six inches from each side.

He mulches with bark, and prunes each plant to a single stem, supporting it with a stake. First fruit is harvested July 4th and he picks continuously into October, frost permitting.

Other advice Mr. Klein gives to the beginner concerns the ripening of fruit. When fruit fails to ripen, it is generally due to lack of phosphorous, an important plant nutrient necessary for seed production. "If the seeds are not formed and reach maturity, the tomato will continue to stay green," says Mr. Klein.

Because he applies fertilizer high in phosphorous, his tomatoes ripen quickly and that accounts for a high continuous yield from July 4th into October.

A lot of gardeners use only manure in the planting area, and do not follow through with additional feedings. Though in many cases the plants will appear to look healthy (too healthy because of so much manure) they may take forever to ripen without phosphorous.

Advice to the Beginner Vegetable Gardener

A newspaper reporter once asked me to list ten golden rules for a successful vegetable garden. Here's how I responded:

1 — **Start small.** Don't try to plant too big a garden the first year. This is the biggest mistake new gardeners make. They see the beautiful seed rack displays or catalog pages with glorious pictures of mouthwatering melons and corn and they try to plant everything. Then, when the weeds start to grow and the days turn hot and humid, they get discouraged and lose interest. It's best to start small with a few easy-to-grow practical salad varieties, then work up in stages to a bigger garden. A small garden managed well will produce more than a large garden badly neglected.

2 — **Start with easy-to-grow varieties.** The easiest to grow varieties of vegetables are beans, onions, radish, looseleaf lettuce, beets, chard, zucchini squash, tomatoes, peppers and cabbage. If you plant zucchini, you needn't plant cucumbers, since baby zucchini squash can serve the same purpose and take up less room. Chard is an excellent substitute for spinach, easier to grow, longer lasting and more tolerant to hot weather. With radish, beans, lettuce and beets don't sow the whole packet at one time. Save some seeds for a second sowing after the first crop is harvested.

3 — **Soil preparation is vital.** A new garden generally will need three important soil preparation steps:

a — Deep digging with removal of stones and fine raking
b — Addition of a soil conditioner such as peat or compost plus liming for acid soils
c — Fertilizer

The most important start you can give to your new garden is to prepare the soil well. Object is to get a fine, level, crumbly soil that drains well.

4 — **Don't overspend on equipment.** For your first garden you could get by with just a spade and a rake, although a hoe and a trowel are useful. When you're ready for a larger vegetable garden — about 1/4 acre or more — a small roto-tiller may be a good investment, but to begin, keep your equipment simple.

5 — **Start a compost pile.** Pile grass clippings, wood ashes, kitchen wastes, weeds and shredded leaves into a corner. Over a period of time the inside of the pile will break down into a dark brown crumbly, humus-rich soil conditioner for spreading on your garden in spring and fall to maintain good soil tilth year after year.

6 — **Use a mulch.** Between rows of vegetables, put down a layer of mulch such as leaves, peat moss, straw, sawdust or black plastic strips. The slight trouble to do this is well worth the benefits:

a — Weed control
b — Moisture conservation
c — Temperature regulation
d — Keeps fruit clean

7 — **Don't neglect your garden.** Only weeds thrive on neglect. It's best to spend a few minutes in your garden at the end of each day before the sun goes down than try to catch up on a week's neglect. If you pull a few weeds each day, run a hoe between the rows to keep the soil loose, and keep an eye open for any early pest damage, you'll find your garden almost takes care of itself. But let the weeds grow, or the pests multiply, and the work of catching up can put a damper on your spirits.

8 — **Try to make your garden a family affair.** One of the most inspiring sights is to see a husband and wife — or a father and son — working together in their garden. Gardening seems to make tensions disappear. Also, two pairs of hands make gardening easier.

9 — **Vegetables need sunlight.** At least six hours direct sunlight a day is necessary for good results with vegetables. While it is possible to have shade gardens of flowers such as impatiens and begonias, there's no such luck with vegetables.

10 — **Don't plant before you should.** Biggest losses of seeds and plants are from setting them out too early. Certain vegetables tolerate cool conditions and need early planting (lettuce, beets, radish, peas, spinach, cabbage) while others are sensitive to cold nights and should not be planted out until all danger of frost is past (tomatoes, peppers, melons, corn and beans, for example).

Question: Seeds that I started indoors germinated well, but after a few days they all wilted and died in spite of good light and moisture. What caused this?

Answer: Your problem is "damping-off" disease. This is a destructive fungus in the soil which attacks seedlings at soil level, causing them to collapse and die. To avoid this happening again use only clean planters, and a soil mixture bought from the store. Do not use garden soil.

(*Above*) *Bibb lettuce grown shoulder-to-shoulder in a "block" planting pattern ensures maximum productivity from available space.*

27

New Vegetable Varieties
to Make Gardening Easier and More Rewarding

Generally speaking, most of the work conducted by vegetable breeders developing new vegetables for the home garden is concentrated on 9 important areas: flavor, yields, earliness, disease resistance, color, space-saving, heat and cold tolerance, size and nutritional value.

Following is my choice of outstanding vegetables which provide best examples of this valuable breeding work on behalf of the home gardener.

Flavor

Flavor is the most important consideration among home gardeners. A new vegetable can have all the disease resistance and nutritional value in the world, but if it lacks good flavor it is not likely to succeed.

It isn't true that home grown vegetable varieties today lack the flavor of old-fashioned kinds. In fact, there are many indisputable examples of superior flavor as a result of modern breeding techniques.

Sweet Corn *Early Xtra Sweet.* New extra-sweet genes are being introduced into sweet corns to make them extra sweet. Sweet Corn *Early Xtra Sweet* won an All-America Award because it is two weeks earlier than *Illini Xtra Sweet* — previously regarded as the sweetest of sweet corns. Compared to other varieties of sweet corn *Early Xtra Sweet* is twice as sweet at harvest, and although it does lose its flavor after picking like other sweet corns it does not lose it so quickly, and 48 hours after picking it is as much as four times sweeter than other corns. To develop its full sweetness there is only one important requirement — it must not be allowed to cross-pollinate with other sweet corn varieties.

Sweet Corn *Silver Queen.* The tenderest, best flavored white corn is *Silver Queen*, growing extraordinary large ears filled right to the tip with tender melt-in-the-mouth milky white kernels. Once you have tried it you'll never want to miss a summer without it. Even if you don't have room in your garden for corn and prefer to buy from a local roadside stand, ask for *Silver Queen* by name. In many areas it has such a loyal following that some growers will only sell to favored customers. It's later than other sweet corns, but well worth the wait and the very best for freezing.

Seedless Watermelons. There's more reason to grow seedless watermelons than the obvious benefit of no seeds. All the plant's energy is directed into producing a more vigorous, healthy vine — and a deep red fruit that's twice as sweet as the other varieties. One variety of seedless watermelon called *Triple Sweet Hybrid* is rated three times as sweet.

Seedless watermelons have been slow to catch on, however, and one reason — according to the breeder — is that people find it hard to believe you can have a seedless watermelon and yet be able to grow them from seed. It's like crossing a jackass onto a mare to produce a mule. The mule is sterile — it produces no seed. It works exactly the same way with seedless watermelons — the seedless fruit is the "mule." They're a little more trouble to grow since they do need another watermelon variety to act as a pollinator in order to set fruit, but that flavor thrill is well worth the extra effort.

Also, the seeds need a little warmer temperature to germinate than normal watermelons, and it's wise to start them indoors in Jiffy-7 peat pellets at 70° F, then transplant to the garden after all danger of frost. Seed companies selling packets of seedless watermelon seed will normally include seed of a pollinator — stained a distinctive color so you can tell them apart.

Lettuce *Buttercrunch* is the most flavorful of all lettuce varieties. It's an All-America award winner that has swept to popularity because of its crisp, buttery taste. The dark outer leaves are delicious enough to eat, but the inner heart of this lettuce is so sweet and crunchy you'll prefer to eat it like an apple. A head lettuce, it can be sown continuously all season — even in hot weather — to produce a steady supply.

Lazy Wife Pole Bean. With the demand for labor-saving, easier-to-grow vegetables it is sad to see that the stately pole bean has fallen out of favor with the steady introduction of numerous new bush beans. Pole beans have superior flavor and are more productive — but they take up a lot of room and people can't be bothered any more to put up poles for supports. Soon, pole beans may disappear from seed catalogs altogether since they are troublesome for seed producers to grow and harvest. In my opinion the best flavored bean in the world is one that seems to have disappeared from nearly all seed catalogs. Called *Lazy Wife,* it grows plump, buttery beans on vines that can be planted in between corn to grow up the stalks to save space and poles.

Apart from being the best bean cooked or baked, it is completely stringless and the older it gets the better it tastes — until the pods dry out completely. It has been dropped from most seed catalogs because of its lateness — but for me that's a benefit since it starts to produce when other bean varieties have finished bearing.

For fear that it may be dropped forever from seed catalogs, I save my own seed each year and treasure them as though they were nuggets of gold.

High Yields

Vegetables noted for heavy yields are especially important to the home vegetable gardener who needs to gain maximum rewards from minimum space. Since most high-yielding vegetables are hybrids they generally cost more than standard varieties, but since the crop they produce can be twice normal yields it's certainly worth paying the extra quarter or 50 cents. Here is my personal selection among the heavy yielding varieties.

Green Arrow Pea. Bred in England, the most famous pea growing nation in the world, *Green Arrow* grows more peas per pod than any other variety. Previously I didn't think peas were worth the space they occupied, but *Green Arrow* now changes my mind on that, averaging nine to 11 peas in each pod. The dark green pods measure five inches in length, and they belong to the wrinkled-seeded class — noted for sweetest flavor. But *Green Arrow* has yet another benefit — it is resistant to both downy mildew and fusarium wilt (two troublesome pea diseases). Never has there been such a remarkable pea — heavy yielding, flavorful and disease resistant all in one. This is modern vegetable breeding expertise at its very best.

Brussels Sprouts, *Jade Cross.* Nowhere in the vegetable kingdom are the benefits of hybridizing more apparant than in *Jade Cross* Brussels Sprouts. Ten days earlier than standard varieties, it grows tall stems 2 ft. high packed solidly from top to toe with tight, dark green sprouts in such abundance that one plant will produce as much as two standard varieties.

Earliness

Earliness is an important consideration when planting a small vegetable garden since this is often an important clue to heavy yields or a longer harvesting period. In other instances it means you can finish one crop in time to plant another to get double-value from the same space.

To determine the relative earliness of different varieties always check the catalog or packet descriptions to see how many days are needed to reach maturity.

Broccoli *Green Comet.* Check any listing of broccoli and you will see that *Green Comet* is 20 days earlier than old-fashioned varieties, and in my opinion that's good enough reason to pay a little extra for. This extra earliness allows *Green Comet* to be grown more successfully as a spring crop — a risky business with other varieties since they cannot tolerate hot weather. After you pick the central head of *Green Comet* numerous side shoots will develop into smaller heads of a deep blue-green and tight bud clusters. The tightness of the heads creates an eating quality that is supreme.

Turnip *Tokyo Cross.* This white, globe-shaped turnip

(*Above*) *Green arrow pea grows 10 peas to the pod, and sometimes as many as 11 peas.*

takes just 35 days to develop its smooth, mild-flavored roots — 15 days ahead of other turnips. These are best eaten when 2 inches across, although they can be left in the ground to grow larger without spoiling. Like *Jade Cross* Brussels sprouts and Broccoli *Green Comet*, Turnip *Tokyo Cross* is a hybrid, and a product of Japanese plant breeding ingenuity.

Carrot *Little Finger*. This cute little carrot is best of the bunch for home gardens since it colors-up and is ready to eat a full 10 days ahead of other carrots. What's more its superb flavor will satisfy the most discriminating gourmet. The flesh is tender, sweet and almost coreless, and is best eaten when the carrot is 3 1/2 inches long. The cylindrical shape makes it an exceptionally fine variety for canning.

Carrot seed is tiny, and a packet normally contains about 1,500 seeds — too many to expect to plant in straight lines. Because of its small size Little Finger is best broadcast in a broad row rather than a straight line, again enabling the small-space gardener to gain maximum yield from his cultivated area.

Disease Resistance

With so much concern over the indiscriminate use of pesticides and fungicides, built-in disease resistance is vitally important — especially among those plants that

29

are susceptible to disease such as cabbage, bush beans and tomatoes.

Tomato Spring Giant. This outstanding early tomato was the first hybrid tomato to win an All-America Award, and although the award was given largely for its high productivity and rich red globular fruit, it is resistant to both verticillium and fusarium wilts, the most common tomato diseases. In many areas of the United States infestation of these diseases is so serious it no longer pays to grow other kinds of tomatoes.

Disease resistance in tomatoes can be recognized by the initials *VFN* after the variety name. The *V* and *F* stand for the above named wilt diseases, while *N* stands for Nematode resistance. Nematodes are microscopic worms that live around plant roots and cause much destruction.

Wax Bean Goldcrop. Resistant to the troublesome bean disease, curly top virus, this new bush snap bean from the United States Department of Agriculture also has greater resistance to blossom drop during hot weather. Goldcrop is an excellent home garden variety, producing long, slender, crisp yellow beans straight as a pencil and full of flavor. It is well deserving of its All-America Award.

New Colors

People often wonder why breeders develop new colors in vegetables, what benefits they have, and is there really any demand for these colorful oddities.

Strangely enough, some of the most popular vegetables are vegetables of a different color.

Sixty years ago there was a fierce prejudice against yellow corn. People believed that white corn was for humans and yellow corn was for cattle. Then along came a yellow corn that changed people's prejudice. Its name was *Golden Bantam*, the sweetest corn of its time and still one of the top selling corns today — 60 years later.

Watermelon Yellow Baby. A happy cross between an American female parent and a Chinese male parent, *Yellow Baby* is a yellow-fleshed hybrid watermelon from China, and winner of an All-America award. The crisp, bright pineapple-yellow flesh is delicious — sweeter than other "icebox" red varieties. It's more productive and just as early to ripen (ready for eating within 70 to 75 days of sowing seed). Also, it has fewer seeds than other "icebox" varieties.

Rhubarb Chard. The crimson stalks of this easy-to-grow green vegetable are highly ornamental, bringing a welcome display of color to the vegetable garden. The luscious mid-ribs can be cooked and served like asparagus with melted butter and breadcrumbs (they taste the same, too). Unlike regular rhubarb, the leaves are not poisonous, and are delicious served as greens.

Royalty Bush Bean. There are two good reasons to consider this purple-podded bush bean in your garden.

First, bean beetles seem to avoid it, and for canning it holds its quality and flavor better than other bush beans. The dark purple color disappears on cooking, and the pods turn an attractive green.

Purple-Headed Cauliflower. The same kind of color change that occurs with *Royalty Bean* takes place with *Purple-Headed Cauliflower* — immediately on cooking it miraculously changes to green. The heads don't require blanching like white cauliflower, and the flavor is more appetizing.

Golden Beet. The best reason to grow this novelty is that it doesn't bleed like red beets, which are notorious for staining salads and main dishes. Also, the golden beet has delicious flavor, and the tops are tastier than red beets, making an excellent substitute for spinach. *White Beets*, too, have similar qualities and well worth consideration in the home vegetable garden.

Space Savers

A great deal of breeding work is being spent to make certain vegetables more compact so they occupy less space — but still give acceptable results.

Romano 14 Bush Bean is an Italian bean, considered to be the best tasting class of green beans. A problem in the past has been the need to support the tall vines on poles. *Romano 14*, however, grows just 18 in. tall, each dwarf bushy plant loaded with the familiar wide, flat Romano-type beans with the same delicious flavor as pole Romanos. This is a wonderful new variety for small home gardens.

Patio Pik Cucumber. Loads of cucumbers grow on dwarf plants that are especially suited for containers. A short trellis is all it needs for support. Also, *Patio Pik* is an all-female variety — although the occasional male flower does grow to act as pollinator. You will have to keep a sharp eye for the males, however, and use a camel's hair brush to pollinate the open female flowers so they bear fruit. You can recognize the females easily — they have baby cucumbers already formed at the base of each flower.

Cinderella Pumpkin is the first bush pumpkin. Instead of growing on sprawling vines that take up loads of room, *Cinderella* matures its fruit on bush-type plants that resemble zucchini squash plants rather than pumpkins.

Bush Acorn Squash Table King is a recent All-America award winner. There have been bush varieties of acorn squash before *Table King*, but the problem with these has been the small fruit size. To get a decent size fruit preferred for meals you still had to grow the vining kinds. *Table King*, however, grows good size fruit on bushy plants with small seed cavities and excellent flavor.

Small Fry Hybrid Tomato is one of several new varieties of dwarf hybrid tomatoes suitable for growing in containers, or as hanging baskets. The cherry size fruit are produced in great quantity, and the plants are disease resistant.

Stonehead Cabbage. When I'm asked to recommend a good cabbage for home gardens it's always *Stonehead* that gets my approval. Bred in Japan, it's an All-America award winner, and it's ideal for home gardens because of its quality and size, allowing for a greater number of cabbage heads per row. Being a hybrid, it has outstanding vigor and uniformity, plus resistance to yellows disease. More important, however, is the fact that each head is just the right size for an average family — growing six inches across, firm and solid. Whereas most other varieties of cabbage require spacing 18 inches to two feet apart, *Stonehead* can be planted close with 12 inches being ample. There are smaller cabbages

than *Stonehead* — notably *Lilliput* and *Tom Thumb* — but for practical purposes they are too small.

Heat & Cold Tolerance

America has two extremes of climate over most of the country — cold sub-zero winters and viciously hot, drenchingly humid summers. Because of this climate range American home gardeners are extremely fortunate since we can grow a far greater variety of fresh vegetables than our counterparts in Canada, Great Britain or other countries of Europe, where cantaloupes cannot grow in the open ground, and even sweet corn and tomatoes have extremely short seasons.

Early Crenshaw Hybrid Melon. For many melon connoisseurs the most exotic melon taste of all is the *Crenshaw*, served in expensive restaurants and shipped from Southern California. It used to be that you could

31

Rhubarb or Ruby Chard is a long lasting, ornamental vegetable, and a heat-resistant substitute for spinach.

Watermelon Yellow Baby is the sweetest flavored early watermelon with 50 per cent fewer seeds than other "icebox" varieties.

Sweet Corn, Early Xtra Sweet is the sweetest flavored sweet corn and two weeks earlier than the next sweetest variety.

Brussels Sprouts Jade Cross is not only the earliest variety of Brussels sprouts, it also has twice the yields of older varieties.

Broccoli Green Comet, an All-America Winner, is up to 20 days earlier than any other variety of broccoli.

Tomato Supersonic is a highly productive variety with the best all-around quality and flavor of any home garden variety.

only grow *Crenshaw* melons in the south and south western states where a long, warm, sunny season allows them to ripen to perfection.

Early Hybrid Crenshaw changes all that. It's early enough for as far north as New York State, where it produces fruits weighing 14 lbs. of firm salmon-pink flesh and smooth yellow-green skins. I once served one of these vine-ripened specimens on a television talk show. "Food of the Gods!" exclaimed the host. My sentiments entirely!

Giant Vegetables

Part of the fun of growing your own vegetables is competing with your neighbors to grow giant-size vegetables. A giant pumpkin or a giant tomato will also bring shrieks of delight from young children. Many vegetables noted for giant size have other qualities also.

Delicious Tomato. There's much more reason to grow *Delicious* tomato than its huge size. Although individual fruit have been known to weigh more than 3 lbs. apiece it can't be beat for good flavor.

Beefsteak has the name in large fruited tomatoes, but it's really *Delicious* that wins every time for large size and meaty flavor. The smooth, red fruits are almost solid meat, with very small seed cavities.

Big Max Pumpkin. If you want to win giant pumpkin growing contests then *Big Max* is the variety to grow. Fruits weighing over 200 lbs. each are commonplace. Flesh is edible, and the exterior skin is a glowing reddish orange unbeatable for Halloween display. Also, the seeds are extra large for roasting.

Mammoth Russian Sunflower. After pumpkins then sunflower growing contests are the next most hotly competitive vegetable growing sport. Heads of *Mam-*

32

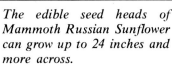

The edible seed heads of Mammoth Russian Sunflower can grow up to 24 inches and more across.

This experimental bush watermelon plant occupying less space than a tomato plant is what home gardeners could be growing in the near future.

Edible podded peas of the future will stay edible even after the peas have started to swell the pods.

Pepper Bell Boy, an All-America winner, grows the highest proportion of four-lobed fruits, excellent for stuffing.

Big Max Pumpkin is the variety to grow when you want to win a pumpkin growing contest.

Gleaming like nuggets of gold this hybrid pepper seed has been screened of pulp and stems and is left to dry prior to storage and packaging into seed packets.

moth Russian grow largest of all — often 25 inches and more in diameter. The seeds, too, are large and edible.
Prizetaker Lima Bean. This should be called "Jack-in-the-Beanstalk" plant. Not only are pods and beans the largest of all limas, the vines will grow to tremendous heights — as much as 50 ft. in one season.

Nutritional Value

All fresh vegetables have greater nutritional value than store-bought kinds since the longer you keep any vegetable the greater the vitamin loss. However, breeders are turning their attention to creating new vegetables with even greater nutritional value.

Caro-Rich Tomato has been developed at Purdue University. Orange-red in color, it has proven to contain 10-times the vitamin *A* content of most other tomatoes.

Other Qualities

Vigor, length of cropping, shape, habit and numerous other qualities are further combinations that breeders can work with in their efforts to improve vegetables.

Zucchini Squash Aristocrat, an All-America winner, bears its fruit upright — off the ground — and the smooth, rounded, glossy dark green slender fruits don't fatten up and spoil as fast as other varieties of zucchini squash.

Cauliflower Self-Blanche. One of the chores involved in growing good quality cauliflower — especially if you want snow-white heads — is to tie the outer flag leaves over the head. *Self Blanche,* however, has been developed with the remarkable characteristic of growing a full head with the leaves already tightly curled over the head.

Pepper Bell Boy. The best peppers of all are those sweet bell peppers with four lobes. This quality gives them perfect shape for stuffing and slicing in salads. *Bell Boy* grows a higher proportion of four lobed fruit than any other pepper, and it is resistant to tobacco mosaic, a common virus disease that destroys peppers.

Edible Soy Beans. High in protein, edible soy beans have a flavor that is sweeter than the oily agricultural soy bean, but they are a problem to shell, since the pods are small, tough to open, and yield only a small number of pea-size beans. The only way to enjoy them is to cook the pods in salt water, then serve hot in a bowl like peanuts. You can then squeeze the pods between thumb and forefinger, and squirt the beans into your mouth. Honestly, there's no better method. We've tried.

Vegetables of the Future

Within the next 5 to 10 years, America may have a new watermelon that takes less space than a tomato vine, capable of yielding up to three fruit weighing 12 lbs. each. Also coming along are bush cucumbers and bush cantaloupes capable of growing impressive yields on compact, bushy plants.

How would you like to grow sweet corn with no cob? — at least not a cob in the accepted sense? It's shaped like a candle, and you eat it like a candy stick. The center is more like a stem, and will easily go through an electric garbage grinder. For freezing it also has advantages since regular size cobs can leach their "woody" flavor through to the kernels.

The "corn-with-no-cob" is another real prospect for the very near future.

Garden peas are due for a big change. Not far ahead is the introduction of "snap peas" — combining the sweet flavor of common garden peas, plus juicy, edible pods like sugar-pod peas. As the peas swell inside the pods and become normal size, the pod walls stay tender unlike existing sugar-pod peas. You eat the peas and the pods raw or cooked, no shelling needed.

Jumbo peas are in the making — each pea the size of a baby lima bean, yet with the sweetness of a "petite pois."

Other super productive vegetables of the future could be all-female melons where all flowers are capable of bearing fruit just like all-female cucumbers which already exist.

From Japan we might see in the future an edible mushroom called Inokedake, which can be grown indoors on a dish of sawdust within two weeks of sowing the spores.

Another surprising newcomer could come from mainland China in the form of a three-in-one vegetable. This sensational new vegetable is heat resistant, takes just 50 to 60 days to mature from seed, and can be eaten three ways. It has a crown of tender, green leaves that can be cooked like spinach, while its thick, central stalk can be peeled and eaten raw like celery or cooked like asparagus.

What else does the future bring? Lots of exciting surprises to be sure. And that, too, is part of the fun of gardening — to read the seed catalogs, search the store displays and hunt through the garden columns for news of the latest from the world's breeding establishments.

Why F₁ Hybrids Are Better

More and more in seed catalogs and seed stores gardeners are seeing new vegetables and flowers described as F1 Hybrids.

The word hybrid comes from the Latin *hybrida,* meaning "offspring of a tame sow and a wild boar." But a much more useful animal hybrid is the mule — the offspring of a jackass and a mare. Combining strength and vigor, the mule has been invaluable to mankind both on the farm and in pioneering.

In the plant world, hybrids are crosses between selected parents of different varieties. The resulting progeny often is worthless and has to be discarded by the plant breeder. But once in a while the result is a new super hybrid that combines strength and vigor just like the mule animal.

Vegetables to Grow in Containers

There's no longer any reason *not* to grow your own vitamin-rich, flavorful, fresh vegetables. Even people without land can have a garden if they really want to. All you need is a doorstep, a windowsill or a sunny balcony. There are vegetables that will even grow in a shady window (mung beans and garden cress).

Bushel baskets, plastic buckets, coffee cans, empty milk cartons, plastic bags and other easily accessible containers are all suitable for raising vegetables. Or use colorful Mexican planters and redwood tubs for extra decorative appeal.

Soil For Containers

Generally speaking, the larger the container the better results you can expect from growing vegetables. More soil depth means less chance of plants drying out unexpectedly. A single plant of tomato, cucumber, pepper, eggplant or chard, for example, should have a container that holds at least 2 quarts of planting soil (a 6 in. clay or plastic pot is equal to 2 quarts of soil mix).

For bush beans, lettuce, carrots, beets, turnips, onions, radish, parsley, herbs and strawberries a balcony planter box 3 ft. long by 8 in. wide by 6 inches deep is sufficient room.

For soil it is best to use a packaged planting mix — such as Jiffy-Mix — available from most garden centers or garden departments. This has the right proportions of sterile planting soil and fertilizer already mixed. However, if you plan on having a large number of containers or raised beds then it will pay to mix your own. In which case, follow this formula:

Blend equal parts *peat* and *vermiculite*. Add to each bushel of mix 4 ounces of pulverized *dolomitic limestone*, 4 ounces of vegetable fertilizer. Mix thoroughly and moisten with water to allow for easier handling.

Containers should have drainage holes in the bottom, and these drainage holes must be covered with cinders, stones or crocks to prevent clogging-up.

Recommended Varieties

Given enough room any variety of vegetable can be grown in containers. However, within families of vegetables there are varieties which are easier to grow this way and more reliable.

Tomatoes. Best tomato varieties for containers are *Tiny Tim* (a small cherry type), *Small Fry* (small cherry), and *Pixie* (slightly larger). There is a larger fruited variety called *Patio*, but it is too late for my liking. Earliest of these is Pixie, but Small Fry is by far the most productive. Also it has disease resistance and is an All-America Winner. In Denmark I have seen *Tiny Tim* sold as an expensive pot plant at Christmas time, and it makes a good hanging basket, growing vines that reach little more than 15 in. To aid pollination "jiggle" plants when flowers appear.

Peppers and Eggplant. These are closely related to tomatoes, and one plant to a 6 in. pot will ensure strong sturdy growth. *Bell Boy* hybrid pepper (an All-America Winner) changes from green to red, while *Sweet Banana* (also an All-America Winner) changes from green to yellow to red. Both are vigorous and decorative, providing good eating and mild flavor.

Growing 25 ins. tall, *Early Beauty Hybrid* eggplant is a good variety for containers. As with peppers and tomatoes, shake plants for pollination.

Cucumber. The new variety called *Patio-Pik* is exceptional for container growing, producing a short, vigorous vine that requires just a short trellis for support (see page 30 for full description).

Zucchini Squash. Any kind of summer squash will grow well in containers, but the zucchini and summer crookneck types are most satisfactory. Grow them in roomy 12 in. pots, or try them as hanging baskets. They cascade effectively, especially planted two or three to a pot, while both flowers and fruit are decorative. Best variety is a recent All-America Winner called *Aristocrat* with handsome, dark green glossy fruits (see page 33 for full description).

Zucchini and crookneck squash produce male and female flowers on the same plant, but since container-grown plants are often out of reach of natural pollinators such as bees, you should try to effect the transfer of pollen with a camel's hair brush to ensure fruit formation.

Rhubarb. For me the variety called *Valentine* is the best to grow in containers because the stalks are brilliant red, decorative and delicious for desserts and pies. Rhubarb is easily grown from seed, although you must wait until at least the second season before you can have stalks large enough to pick. For quicker results it's possible to buy mature roots.

Containers for rhubarb must be equivalent to a 12 in. pot, allowing adequate room for vigorous root development. They are gross feeders, and will benefit from generous quantities of decomposed manure or compost. A bushy, well grown rhubarb plant is as decorative as any foliage plant.

Root Vegetables. Citrus crates or any deep wooden boxes will provide adequate space for radish, beets, carrots and turnips, especially the smaller-rooted varieties that can be grown close together. Carrot *Little Finger* is a superb miniature carrot ideal for this purpose. The short, slender, orange-red roots are edible about 10 days ahead of other carrot varieties, and they taste superb — a gourmet's delight. Plant two rows in a 3 ft. balcony planter, spacing carrots 2 in. apart.

Among turnip varieties, *Tokyo Cross* is the best choice for containers. It's not only 15 days earlier than other turnips, it is best eaten when just 2 in. across — although it will continue to grow much larger without spoiling. Turnips and radish need similar conditions — a cool growing period. They don't do well in hot weather. Give same spacing as carrots.

Beets sown in planter boxes can be sown thickly and picked young the size of golf-balls. *Ruby Queen* is a good variety and an All-America Winner. Give same spacing as carrots.

Lettuce. Of the great many leaf vegetables suitable for container gardening, lettuce is perhaps the most desirable, and here we have an infinite choice. First I must recommend *Oak Leaf,* which is especially good for containers because you don't have to pick the whole plant to make a serving of salad. Pick the outer leaves of several plants, and more inner leaves will grow to take their place. Also, it's more heat resistant than other lettuce varieties. A 3 ft. balcony planter will hold eight plants spaced 4 ins. apart.

Ruby lettuce has reddish, frilled leaf edges, creating a decorative effect in a container, while *Salad Bowl* grows an enormous mound of frilly green leaves equally decorative and delicious. Both are All-America winners.

All the foregoing lettuce varieties are the looseleaf type — easiest to grow and earliest. *Buttercrunch* is the best flavored of the head lettuce, and there are several good miniature varieties to consider — notably *Tom Thumb.*

Spinach is easily grown in containers. Just ensure that you sow the seed to mature during the cool weather of spring or fall. *Malabar spinach* is heat resistant, and although it does create a long, leafy vine you can take cuttings and root them in water to create an ornamental indoor plant hanging from a bottle. Give regular spinach same spacing as lettuce.

Chard is a good spinach substitute, enduring hot humid conditions with ease, and the red-stalked *Ruby Chard* is particularly attractive. Grow in a balcony planter spaced 6 ins. apart or in individual 6 in. pots.

Herbs of many kinds will grow in containers, and frankly it is often the best way to grow them in order to keep them within bounds. *Parsley, Chives* and *Mint* are all eminently suitable for growing in containers. Chives and mint will thrive in a coffee can, while parsley makes a stunning pot plant or hanging basket — especially the fine-curled kind. For parsley and chives during winter sow the seed in June or July and give plenty of sunlight.

Of all leafy vegetables, however, *Garden Cress* is unquestionably the easiest to grow and fastest to mature in containers. It is one of the few vegetables that will thrive in a window with a northern exposure. Once you water the seeds you can't *stop* them from germinating. Like mung beans the seed coat splits almost immediately and within 24 hours a shoot appears. Ten days later the cress is ready to trim with scissors for use as a

garnish on salads, sandwiches or egg dishes.

Although this is largely a chapter on growing vegetables in containers, I must make mention of dwarf fruit trees you can grow in a tub. One is a remarkable mini-peach called *Bonanza* and the other is a mini nectarine called *Nectarina.* If you have room in a sunny location for a 12 in. pot or redwood tub you can grow it. The fruit are regular size, sweet and juicy, but the trees never grow more than 4 to 5 ft. high. In spring they bear beautiful blossoms, followed by large full-size fruit in summer.

In the small-fruit category strawberries will add double-delight to your patio or balcony, creating a decorative effect — and bearing fruit. I especially recommend the alpine strawberry, *Baron Solemacher,* because of its "wild strawberry" flavor — yet twice the size of wild strawberries. Easily grown from seed to bear the first year, it stays neat and compact since it does not produce runners.

This is by no means a complete evaluation of vegetables and fruit for growing in containers. Bush beans, endive and onions are obvious additions. I have even seen three ears of corn growing tall and sturdy from a metal bucket with a cluster of dwarf French marigolds and white alyssum spilling over the sides for decorative effect.

Breeders, too, are devoting a good deal of attention to creating more compact varieties of vegetables — increasing the number of varieties suitable for containers. It's possible, for example, that a dwarf cantaloupe and bushy watermelon may be on the horizon.

Some people may scoff at growing vegetables in containers or indoors, pointing out that by the time you've taken into consideration cost of pots and fertilizers for these small plantings the savings over store-bought vegetables are unrealistic. However, there's more to growing vegetables in containers than saving money — otherwise why would anyone grow house plants?

Vegetables for Ornamental Value

One of the most memorable sights of a recent trip to Europe was touring the gardens of Versailles Palace in France and stumbling across a cluster of cottage gardens planted for ornamental effect with green cabbages and a border of marigolds.

It was a beautiful sight to see the round, uniform cabbages looking like gigantic green rose buds and creating such an interesting ornamental effect. Ever since I've kept a special eye open for other ornamental ideas using vegetables. Here are a few of the best.

Ruby Chard is exceptionally attractive when planted in containers. The thick brilliant red leaf stalks and dark crinkled leaves stay colorful and decorative all summer. Use it as a highlight in flower borders also.

Lettuce often can be ornamental — especially Ruby with its red tinged leaves and Salad Bowl with its frilly foliage. Plant them in window boxes mixed with flowering annuals, and as an edging in the flower border.

Parsley and many other herbs make attractive edgings to a flower border. Parsley is good to mix with annuals in container plantings and it makes an attractive hanging basket in full sun providing you resist the temptation to cut too many sprigs. Sage, chives and thyme are other herbs that are good for edging and clumps in perennial borders. Horehound is good to plant in a rockery or dry wall.

Tomatoes at one time were grown *only* for ornamental value since they were thought to be poisonous. Best for ornamental effect are the determinate cherry types and the yellow pears. Grow them in containers, window boxes and as hanging baskets.

36

Peppers offer such decorative value that certain kinds have been specially developed for ornamental effect, but these are generally too hot to be edible. Sweet bell peppers that turn red or golden yellow when ripe will look most attractive, and also the yellow banana kind.

Squash come in all kinds, some more decorative than others. The *Yellow Zucchini, Yellow Crooknecks* and *Gold Nugget* are attractive in containers and hanging

baskets, and of course *Turk's Turban* is the one widely grown for ornamental decoration, although its unattractive sprawling vines have no ornamental value.

Beans. Of the many beans that can be considered ornamental, perhaps the best is *Scarlet Runner,* which makes a decorative vine covered in brilliant red flowers.

Sunflowers, of course, have massive flowers and are good to use sparingly as a tall, towering background plant and in groups.

When the subject is ornamental value, the old saying that beauty is in the eye of the beholder, rings true. I have even seen malabar spinach used as an indoor plant vining from a bottle, and in English cottage gardens a brilliant red spinach commands respect in the flower border.

(*Above*) *Bronze-leafed Ruby lettuce and scarlet-ribbed Rhubarb chard create a distinctive ornamental effect in this vegetable garden, as well as being good to eat.*

(*Left below*) *Assortment of large ornamental squash which can be grown as a mixture, all of which are edible. Other popular decorative vegetables are inedible ornamental small-fruited gourds, and bottle gourds which can be dried to make bird nesting boxes and dippers.*

(*Left*) *Close-up view of a Turk's Turban Gourd shows the distinctive bizarre markings which make it highly ornamental for Thanksgiving and Halloween displays.*

37

How to Grow
Your Favorite Vegetables

ARTICHOKE

More misconceptions surround the growing of artichokes than any other vegetable. The globe artichoke is the one used extensively in French cooking dipped in melted butter. They are related to thistles, and form large thistle-like bud clusters surrounded by fleshy scales, which are edible at the base. The closer you get to the center, the more tender and succulent they become.

Jerusalem artichokes, on the other hand, are not even distantly related. They are wild sunflowers or helianthus, growing underground tubers which can be cooked like potatoes. They are hardy, extremely invasive, as well as being tall (6 ft.) and demand a great deal of room. Definitely not recommended for small gardens.

Two plants of globe artichokes are plenty for an average family, and require planting 3 ft. apart.

Like asparagus and rhubarb, artichokes are perennials, living from year to year in areas with mild winters. They do well in sunny coastal areas where a cool climate encourages good bud development, and in the south where they can mature during early spring.

In north east sections of the country they are generally a disappointment, giving only small production during cool fall weather.

Although they can be grown from seed started indoors six weeks ahead of transplanting into the garden after all danger of frost, they are best grown from root divisions in a fertile soil high in nitrogen and given plenty of moisture. Even in good artichoke-growing areas the bud production from first year's growth is generally small (5 or 6 heads) but will increase the second season to 40 or 50.

Pick flower buds when they are two to four inches across and before the scales start to spread open. Left to mature the bud will produce a purple flower head resembling a giant thistle. Dried, they are excellent for use in dried flower arrangements.

ASPARAGUS
If You Have the Room

One of the joys of spring is the magnificent sight of plump, juicy asparagus spears striking through the soil, begging to be snipped and served up at the dinner table cooked with a main dish or raw in salads.

Asparagus is easy to grow, and a bed of it once established and kept fertile will remain productive indefinitely. This delicious spring vegetable has some definite needs, however.

Most important is a *rich, loose soil*, well drained and in an open, sunny position. To get the really plump spears as thick as your thumb plenty of soil conditioner such as well-decomposed compost or manure in the soil is helpful, plus the addition of a vegetable fertilizer. Also, asparagus *cannot tolerate weeds*, and a good policy is to spread a mulch of straw or shredded leaves over the row or bed each spring.

Planting is best done during early spring with large, one-year old roots available from most good garden centers or seed catalogs. The roots are long and plump, resembling an octopus. Dig a trench about 12 ins. wide by 12 ins. deep, filling the bottom 4 inches with a mound of humus enriched soil and vegetable fertilizer. Spread the roots 12 ins. apart like a star and cover with a further 4 ins. of soil. As the young asparagus shoots penetrate the first 4 ins. of soil, fill in the rest of the trench. Since asparagus prefers a lime soil, an 8 oz. dressing of lime per square yard is not excessive and can be repeated each spring.

A light cutting of stalks may be possible the following spring, but it usually takes three-year plants to produce a really good crop. Asparagus grows easily from seed — if you can wait three years — and a packet will normally plant a 20 ft. row.

Cutting begins in early spring and continues until late June, using a sharp knife to cut the stalks on a diagonal just below the soil surface. Small shoots should be allowed to grow until fall when they dry up and can be cut down.

Asparagus is not a space-saving vegetable, and it's best to find a separate bed away from the regular vegetable patch, planting 12-15 roots per person.

Mary Washington is a recommended variety — introduced some 30 years ago as the first disease-resistant variety.

Not recommended for small gardens, artichokes need a fertile soil boosted with a vegetable fertilizer application in spring and fall. A covering of mulch is also necessary for winter protection except in mild areas.

To gain asparagus spears as thick as this the essentials are a weed-free bed and an application of vegetable fertilizer twice a year — in spring and fall. Liming is necessary in acid soil areas.

Clumps of Mary Washington asparagus spears bursting through the soil. Get to them early in the day, since they soon shoot up into a long stalk and lose the juicy, tender flavor. Cut asparagus spears at soil level on a diagonal, using a sharp knife.

(*Top, left*) *Artichoke bud ready for picking* (*left*) *and artichoke flower* (*right*), *well past the edible stage.*

(*Above, left*) *Cauliflower Snow Crown, the earliest "Snowball" type cauliflower, and an All-America winner.*

40

(*Above, center*) *When you grow all-female cucumbers like these, you can expect nearly double normal yields, since the percentage of fruit-bearing female flowers is almost doubled.*

(*Right*) *Yellow-podded pole bean is more trouble to grow than bush kinds, but yields are higher than bush beans, and the flavor is generally considered to be better.*

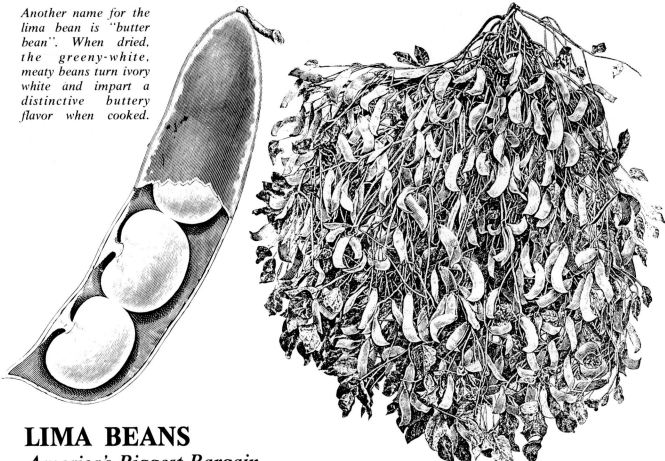

Another name for the lima bean is "butter bean". When dried, the greeny-white, meaty beans turn ivory white and impart a distinctive buttery flavor when cooked.

LIMA BEANS
America's Biggest Bargain

The modern bush lima bean could easily claim distinction as America's biggest bargain. The most popular bush lima bean grown today is the famous *Fordhook Lima Bean*, growing regular-size lima beans on short, bushy plants which require no staking.

How many people realize, however, that when the forerunner to the *Fordhook Lima Bean* was first introduced in 1890 it sold at a packet price of 75 cents *for four beans*. Today — more than 80 years later — you can buy the same kind of beans at a cost of 50 cents for 50 beans. That's about 18 times cheaper today than they were 80 years ago. How many other products today can make the same kind of claim?

Bush lima beans are a worthwhile crop for home gardens since the beans are extra large, meaty, and the kind to eat as "butter beans" when dried. When freshly cooked they have a whitish-green tint and make a delicious meal. Dried, they turn ivory white and store well for winter use.

Limas should be planted well after danger of frost in a fertile soil with good tilth. Their greatest enemy is a cold, wet spell which rots the seed. They require a longer growing season than regular snap beans — about 75 days minimum, while pole limas require two weeks longer. They need full sun, and to get a good stand seeds can be sown close together — 3 ins. apart — but thinned to 8 in. apart, planting the seeds 1 in. deep. Allow 2 ft.

(Above) Here's what a bush lima bean is capable of yielding, given a fertile soil with good tilth and adequate moisture during dry spells. This plant, etched from a photograph, yielded more than 300 pods.

between rows. During dry periods they should be watered heavily, and in order to conserve moisture a mulch of straw or similar material is helpful. A packet will normally sow a 30 ft. row.

Pole lima beans need much more room, and they are capable of reaching unbelievable heights — as much as 50 ft. However, 10 ft. poles in tripod fashion are normally adequate, setting six to eight seeds around each pole. *Prizetaker* is the best variety for growing up poles.

Since the original bush limas were introduced improvements have been made by breeders, and today *Fordhook 242* is the best variety, and the only bush lima to win an All-America award.

It's quite an experience, however, to sit down to your first meal of bush lima beans and to realize that if you were a gardener in 1890 each bean was worth nearly 20 cents, and a mouthful could represent $1.00. In this world of rampant inflation it is some comfort to realize what a bargain seeds really are.

41

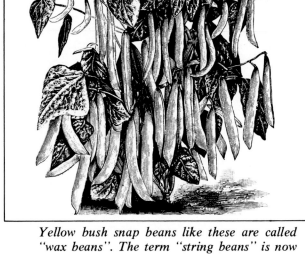

Yellow bush snap beans like these are called "wax beans". The term "string beans" is now outmoded, since breeders bred out the offending strings many years ago.

SNAP BEANS
No More Strings

After tomatoes, snap beans are the most popular vegetable grown in home gardens, and they are much easier to grow. Some people still persist in calling them "string beans", but breeders long ago bred the strings right out of beans, so it's not correct to call them that any more.

Basically, you have bush beans and pole beans. Generally speaking the pole beans are better flavored and more productive, but bush beans have the advantage of being earlier, requiring no poles for support, and they are space-saving.

Among both types there are green-podded and yellow-podded varieties, but an unusual purple-podded bush variety called *Royalty* is worth growing apart from its distinctive color — see page *30* for full description. Also, there are different colored beans. White is the most common, but hunting through several seed catalogs will reveal black-seeded, red-seeded and speckled-seeded varieties, while a variety called *Cherokee Wax* has edible yellow pods and shiny black seeds — a beautiful combination, and fine for making black bean soup.

Kentucky Wonder is the most famous green-podded pole bean, but *Romano* (Italian beans) are considered to be better-flavored. There is a new bush form of Italian bean called *Romano 14*, growing just 18 in. tall, and well worth space in the small garden (see page 30 for full description).

Planting of all varieties is best done directly into the garden after all danger of frost. For the small home gardener rows of bush beans should be spaced 18 ins. apart, planting seed 1 in. deep and 2 in. apart. When the plants are several inches high you can thin them to 4 in.

42

apart. A packet will normally sow a 30 ft. row. Given a good tilth to the soil snap beans will tolerate a wide range of soil conditions.

Every gardener develops his own method of planting pole beans, but whatever the method the aim is to make them grow lush and tall. The hill method is as good as any, digging generous holes and filling with well-decomposed compost, manure or a packaged soil conditioner and a vegetable fertilizer. Then position three poles around the edge to form a tripod and create a bean "wigwam".

Recommended bush snap beans are *Tendercrop* (green pods with purple mottled seeds) and *Goldcrop*, an All-America winner (yellow pods with white seeds).

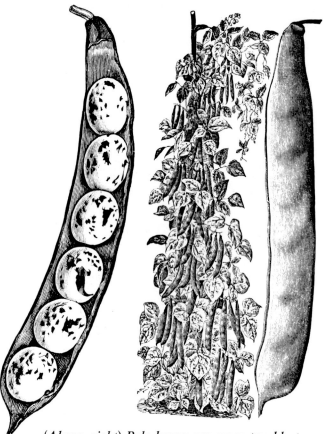

(Above, right) Pole beans are more trouble to grow since they need sturdy supports, but this old fashioned variety called "Lazy Wife" is well worth it. The best flavored of all beans, it is extremely late and has no disease resistance whatsoever. For this reason few seed catalogs continue to list it, but once you've tasted the plump, meaty, buttery beans you'll never be without it in your garden.

(Above, left) Wren's Egg horticultural bean — used mainly for dried beans — has green pods and highly ornamental beans colored white with red speckles like a wren's egg. Black beans and red (kidney) beans are also ornamental when shelled.

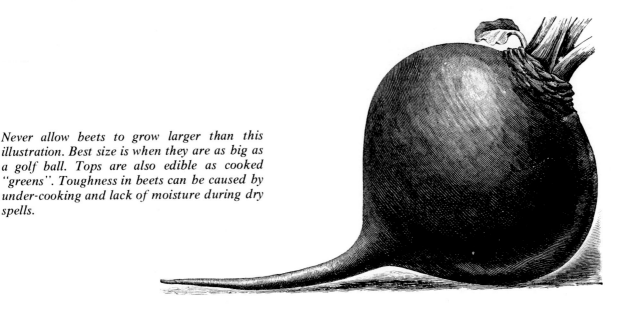

Never allow beets to grow larger than this illustration. Best size is when they are as big as a golf ball. Tops are also edible as cooked "greens". Toughness in beets can be caused by under-cooking and lack of moisture during dry spells.

BEETS
The Two-Purpose Vegetable

Beets are a valuable two-purpose vegetable for small gardens — first for their tasty round roots and second for their edible green tops to substitute for spinach. Enjoy the roots boiled whole as baby or "Harvard" beets, sliced, diced — or cold in salads. Beets are also the prime ingredient of *Borsch*, the famous Russian beet soup. Pickled they are superb, and they will *store over winter* in a box of moist sand in a cool, dark basement. Roots can be harvested from the garden *into December* over most of the country by applying a heavy mulch of straw or similar material.

It's hard to fail with beets, since they tolerate a wide range of soil and climate conditions - providing the soil has *good tilth*. Get a good germination stand and Mother Nature should take care of the rest, although plenty of moisture is necessary for continuous growth. During dry spells they will stubbornly sit still unless watered copiously.

Sow beet seed 1/2 in. deep in rows, covering with fine soil, and thinning the seedlings to 3 inches apart. Although 18 ins. is normally recommended between rows, for small gardens *it's possible to plant two or three rows shoulder-to-shoulder* with just 4 ins. between rows. This way you plant a 1 ft. broad row capable of growing 180 beets best eaten when they reach the size of a golf ball.

The seedlings tolerate light frost, and should be sown in spring 4 weeks before the last frost date in your area. Another sowing in June and a final one in August will ensure a regular supply since beets take only 60 days to develop. A packet of seed will normally plant a 30 ft. row.

Recommended varieties are *Ruby Queen*, the only red beet to win an All-America award, and Burpee's *Golden Beet*.

Although red beets are by far the most popular kinds grown in home gardens, yellow beets and white beets are also worth consideration, since they do not "bleed" like red beets.

43

Brussels sprouts need a long growing season and cool conditions. The edible green sprouts grow all along the central stem, and taste best after a light frost.

(Right) The head of a Cauliflower is called the "curd". It is surrounded by jacket leaves which can be folded over the head and tied to give the cauliflower its clean, crisp "snowball" color.

BROCCOLI & CAULIFLOWER
Cool Weather Crops

The key to success with both broccoli and cauliflower is to time plantings so they mature in *cool weather.* This is especially important of cauliflower, which is best planted as a fall crop, except in high altitude areas where cooler conditions in summer are more favorable.

Raw cauliflower makes a crunchy dip, and a whole head cooked with cheese sauce on top is a famous gourmet dish to serve four people. Choice heads of cauliflower are worth a dollar and more per head, so it pays to grow your own.

Both cauliflower and broccoli will succeed in a wide range of soils with good drainage and good fertility. Well decomposed compost or similar soil conditioner, and a packaged vegetable fertilizer are advisable. Although seeds can be sown outdoors and thinned, it is best to start plants indoors in Jiffy-7 peat pellets, hardened off in a cold frame and transplanted to the garden four weeks before your last frost date. For fall crops start the seed in June and transplant into the garden in July, watering well during dry spells. Space the plants 1-1/2 ft. apart in rows 2 ft. wide.

Cauliflower and broccoli are good crops to follow peas, which generally finish bearing at the end of June. As heads of cauliflower mature, pull the flag leaves over the head and secure with a rubber band to blanche them pure white and protect from early frost damage.

Recommended varieties are *Green Comet* Broccoli, the earliest of all broccoli (see page 29 for full description) and Cauliflower *Snow Crown*, the latest cauliflower to win an All-America award.

A packet of broccoli and cauliflower seed is normally sufficient to sow 150 plants, but a 15 ft. row of 12 plants is adequate for a family of four.

BRUSSELS SPROUTS
Most Valuable Crop

Over most areas of the United States Brussels sprouts are best grown as a fall crop, and since they are the hardiest of all members of the cabbage family they can be harvested right up to Christmas, producing flavorful fresh greens at a time when store prices for fresh produce are at their highest.

As a cost-saving vegetable they are second only to tomatoes, and deserve much greater popularity. The flavor of the sprouts is actually improved after a light frost, and since they must have a long growing season seed should be started in Jiffy-7 peat pellets in June for transplanting out into the garden in July, spaced 18 ins. apart in rows 2 ft. apart, although a 15 ft. row with 12 plants is adequate for a family of four - especially if the variety used is *Jade Cross*. This remarkable hybrid is sometimes the only variety featured in catalogs any more, and a full description is on page 29.

For maximum productivity pinch out the growing tip when the lower sprouts have reached picking size. This will ensure that the rest of the sprouts will mature all along the stem. A fertile soil is also essential.

CABBAGE
Choice of Four Kinds

There are four important kinds of cabbage — green cabbage, red cabbage, savoy cabbage and Chinese cabbage, each with its own distinctive qualities. Green cabbage makes excellent cole slaw and sauerkraut, adds good flavor to salads when shredded, and is good simply boiled or added to soups.

Everything you can say about a green cabbage is true of a red cabbage, plus it makes the best pickle.

Savoy cabbage has rich deep green, textured leaves and a heart of gold. It is considered the very best flavored of all cabbage — and it is highly ornamental because of its crinkled leaves.

In flavor, Chinese cabbage seems to be a cross between a Cos lettuce and a cabbage. In fact it can be served like lettuce in salads or as a nest for hors d'oeuvres, but is best grown as a fall crop sown into the garden in July.

Cabbage demands a well dug, fertile soil, and plenty of moisture during dry spells. Biggest enemies of cabbage are insect pests, attacking the leaves and heart. In the small garden you can generally avoid serious damage by keeping a sharp eye for early signs of trouble. Dispose of eggs and small colonies of insects before they have a chance to multiply. Aphids, slugs and cabbage worms are worst offenders, but it's incredible how much protection a vegetable dust or wood ashes can provide.

Although cabbage seed will germinate readily when sown directly into the garden it is better to start seeds indoors in Jiffy-7 peat pellets, and transplant to the garden four weeks before your last frost date. For fall crops start seed in June and transplant into the garden in July.

Space smaller cabbage such as *Stonehead* 12 inches apart with 18 inches between rows. Larger varieties need spacing 18 ins. apart. A packet of seed will normally grow 125 plants, and needs sowing 1/4 in. deep. For small gardens, to take maximum advantage of space, it's possible to sow varieties like *Stonehead* in rows 12 ins. apart by planting in a diamond pattern.

Recommended varieties are *Stonehead*, growing 15 heads in a 15 ft. row (see page 31 for full description), *Ruby Ball* (dark red, standing in the garden a month before bursting), *Savoy King* (a vigorous hybrid) and *Michihili Chinese cabbage*.

(Top, right) Hard, round cabbage heads like this are the hallmark of a good cabbage. Today, few cabbages will do this more reliably than a family-size hybrid called "Stonehead".

(Below) Savoy cabbages like the one shown here have the reputation of being the most flavorful.

45

GOLDEN BALL

EARLY SCARLET HORN.

OXHEART.

CHANTENAY

TRUE DANVERS.

SAINT VALERY

LONG ORANGE

Carrots come in shapes and sizes to suit every need. Many of these old fashioned varieties have been superceded by modern improved breeding which has resulted in earlier varieties, smaller central "cores", and higher nutritional value.

(Above) In addition to white-ribbed chard there is a highly ornamental red-ribbed kind excellent for growing in containers.

CARROTS
All Shapes and Sizes

Carrots are an amazingly versatile vegetable. Eat them raw — whole like a candy stick or shredded for salad mixing. Sliced or cubed they make a tasty cooked meal, while carrot wine, carrot juice, carrot marmalade and carrot cookies are less familiar ways to enjoy this splendid root crop.

Carrots come in all shapes and sizes to suit your soil conditions. Long slender carrots like *Imperator* and *Spartan Bonus* need a good depth of loose, light soil, while varieties like *Oxheart* and *Little Finger* require less depth. Well decomposed garden compost or a soil conditioner can improve heavy soils for carrots, but to avoid mis-shapen roots clear the soil thoroughly of weed roots and stones.

The biggest mistake made with carrots is allowing the soil to "crust" after the seeds are sown. Carrot seed is small and light. The slightest crusting of soil will seriously impair germination, so it is a good idea to sow the seed just 1/4 in. deep and cover with very fine soil kept moist until the seeds germinate. In cool weather germination is sometimes slow, but the young seedlings are hardy, and can be sown four weeks before the last frost date in your area, thinning the young plants to stand 2 ins. apart. Although rows should be spaced 12 ins. apart, a variety like *Little Finger* can be planted much closer together — as close as 4 ins., creating three lines in a broad 1 ft. row. A packet of seed will contain about 1,500 seeds — enough to plant two or three 15 ft. rows.

Little Finger is a highly recommended variety since it is the earliest of all carrots (10 days ahead of most), and the flavor is superb. See page 29 for full description.

CELERY

Home gardeners seem to have more trouble over growing celery than any other vegetable. The problem is that celery demands a long growing season, offering a greater opportunity for things to go wrong. Also, it demands plenty of moisture and a fertile soil.

Celery adds delicious flavor to soups. Eat raw with a sprinkling of salt or try the stalks braised with fried onions for a delicious side-dish.

Since celery needs an abnormally long growing season, it is best grown as a fall vegetable, sowing seed 1/4 inch deep in rows spaced 12 inches apart. Seed germinates slowly unless soaked in warm water for 24 hours, and most varieties require four months to mature. Transplanting from a seed bed or seed box is also recommended.

To grow the thick, crisp stems to perfection, fertile soil is essential. For celery it should be rich, moist, but well drained, and supplemented with plenty of manure, or compost and a vegetable fertilizer.

There are green stalked and yellow varieties (called self-blanching). *Summer Pascal* needs blanching to develop its best flavor by wrapping newspaper collars around the stems to exclude light or the old method of "earthing-up" around the stalks after they have developed. Self-blanching, yellow stemmed varieties are offered by some seed companies and also green stemmed celery which is eaten without blanching. However, blanching definitely improves the flavor and texture.

Celery seed is tiny, and a packet will normally produce 500 plants; although a 15 ft. row is adequate for a family of four, producing 15 clumps. Plenty of moisture (but not a waterlogged soil) is the real secret of successful celery growing.

46

(*Above*) *Cabbage Emerald Cross, an All-America winner, is the handsomest, largest cabbage you can grow.*

(*Below*) *Green celery is much better for you because it has more nutritional value, but "blanched" celery still has an inimitable flavor and texture that makes "blanching" worth the extra trouble.*

CHARD
Long Lasting and Hardy

Chard is possibly the easiest vegetable of all to grow in your garden. Use the dark green crinkled leaves as boiled "greens", and the thick, succulent stems as substitutes for cooked asparagus — served with melted butter and breadcrumbs.

The more you pick the outer leaves of chard, the more new inner leaves will form in the center to take their place. They tolerate a wide range of climate conditions — from light frosts to savage heatwaves. Nothing except a heavy freeze will deter them, and they can be relied upon to stay productive into December. A heavy straw mulch may help keep them productive even longer.

Sow seeds directly into your garden four weeks before your last frost date. Plant the seeds 1/2 in. deep in rows 18 inches apart, and thin the seedlings to stand at least 6 inches apart. One packet will normally plant a 25 ft. row - although a 15 ft. row is ample for a family of four.

Two kinds of chard are popular - *Fordhook Giant* with thick white stalks, and *Rhubarb* or *Ruby Chard* with crimson stalks. For a really unusual effect try alternating one of each in your vegetable garden.

47

(Top) *Yellow sweet corn still is the most popular, but it didn't use to be that way. At the turn of the century white corn was for humans, and yellow corn was for cattle. Then along came Golden Bantam which proved to be sweeter than any white corn, and gradually changed people's prejudice.*

However, the tables may turn again, since a new white corn called Silver Queen is so good it is making many converts back to white corn.

As a yellow corn, Golden Bantam has been superceded by many excellent new hybrids such as Early Xtra Sweet, possessing extra sweet genes. When you compare the flavor of Early Xtra Sweet with Golden Bantam you will wonder how Golden Bantam could ever have been considered the sweetest corn of its time.

(Left) *Ornamental corn is strictly decorative. Called Indian corn, the kernels are too tough and pasty to be considered good eating.*

SWEET CORN
Sweet, Sweeter, Sweetest

By now everyone should know that the only way to enjoy really delicious corn is to grow your own and have the water boiling as you pick it fresh from the garden. Sweet corn begins to convert its sugar content into starch the moment it is picked, and most varieties will lose 50% of their flavor within 12 hours of leaving the corn stalk.

Another amazing phenomenon about sweet corn is that the wild variety is now extinct. With all other vegetables it is possible to trace their origins to wild species in certain parts of the world. Watermelons, for example, are indigenous to the Kalahari Desert, South Africa, where they can still be found growing with wild abandon. Wild sweet corn has never been found, although it is thought to have originated in Mexico since it was a food staple of the Mayan and Inca civilizations.

In sweet corns, gardeners everywhere seem to demand two important qualities — sweetness first and early ripening second. So with these two considerations in mind we take no hesitation in recommending two super sweet varieties — one early and one late. They are *Early Xtra Sweet*, the sweetest flavored of all yellow corns (see page 28 for full description) and *Silver Queen*, the finest quality white corn (see page 28 for full description).

Corn is not a space-saving vegetable. For decent yields you will need several 15 ft. rows spaced 2 ft. apart. Plant seed 2 ins. deep, 2 ins. apart after all danger of frost, thinning seedlings down to at least 6 ins. A rich soil with good tilth, and plenty of moisture during dry spells are the prime ingredients for successful sweet corn production. Also, remember that sweet corn is pollinated by wind blowing pollen from the tassles on top of the plant to the silks half-way down the stalk, and therefore several short rows are better than one long row.

A serious sweet corn problem is a fungus disease called "smut", creating a black growth which bursts and distorts the developing ears. There is no cure for it, and it is extremely difficult to get rid of, except to burn stalks as soon as it shows itself.

A packet of sweet corn seed will normally plant 100 ft.

Where does sweet corn come from? That's one of nature's most closely guarded secrets since no-one has ever been able to find corn growing in the wild.

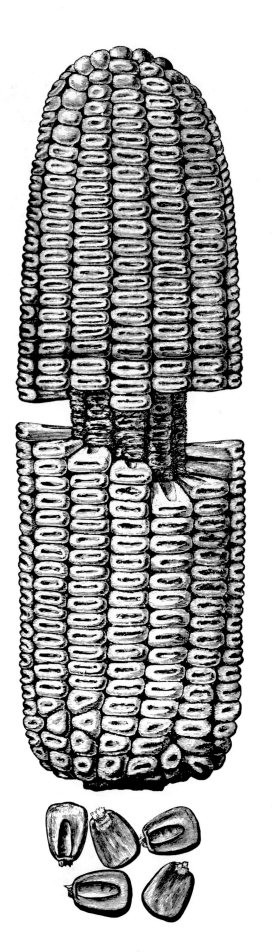

49

CUCUMBER
Effeminate and Burpless

What modern plant breeders have done to the cucumber is astonishing, creating not only all-female and disease resistant varieties, but also bitter-free and burpless varieties.

If you haven't yet tried the new kinds of all-female cucumbers you're in for a nice surprise. Normally in a cucumber there is an over-abundance of male flowers, and it seems like an eternity before that first cucumber-bearing female flower comes along. With the new all-female cucumbers nearly *all* the flowers are capable of producing fruit. Yields are therefore nearly double those of standard cucumbers, and you can thank a plant-finding expedition to Korea for finding the source of the "all-female" character. For successful pollination you either must keep careful watch for the occasional male flower where hand pollination with a camel's hair brush is necessary, or plant a normal bisexual cucumber vine for every three all-females.

Best of the all-female cucumbers for small gardens is *Patio-Pik*, a dwarf variety that can be grown up a short trellis (see page 30 for full description).

Then we have the new "Burpless" cucumbers, which are also best grown up trellis, and can be eaten raw like a candy stick — skin and all.

Of the smaller pickling cucumbers *Wisconsin SMR* is a heavy yielder with disease resistance, and the round variety called *Lemon* is equally good for pickling as well as being deliciously mild flavored.

Cucumbers are best direct-sown into the garden after all danger of frost, although many gardeners prefer to start them in Jiffy-7 peat pellets to get that extra earliness. Plant seeds 1 inch deep in groups of six seeds, later thinning to one healthy vine. Grown up trellis they can be spaced 2 ft. apart, but left to sprawl on the ground they need spacing 4 ft. apart. For small gardens a 15 ft. row grown up trellis is ample for a family of four, giving room for up to 8 plants easily averaging 10 cucumbers each. Keep fruit picked as they mature and more will grow to take their place.

A soil of good tilth is essential, enriched with well-decomposed manure or compost. In addition it's good to use a packaged vegetable fertilizer. Strips of black plastic will make a good mulch, since this will help to absorb heat into the soil to produce earliest crops.

A packet of hybrid cucumber will normally contain 30 seeds.

Basically, cucumbers come in two kinds — slicing cucumbers and pickling. But breeders have made some remarkable improvements in both types that pose the question — what next lies ahead for the cool cucumber?

50

(Right) Cucumbers don't have to be left to sprawl along the ground. You can grow them up poles or strings like this hybridizer, who finds that coffee cans are plenty large enough to grow them in, providing they are well-fertilized.

EGGPLANT
Black is Beautiful

"A bowling ball on a pepper plant" is the best description I ever heard of an eggplant. There is a famous Greek dish called Mousakka, a baked vegetable casserole, made from minced meat, cheese, potatoes and eggplant. Without the eggplant this dish would hardly live up to its reputation. For this reason alone it is worth growing, although eggplant fritters are a great favorite during summer.

Related to peppers, eggplant has a similar bushy, compact growth habit, and it thrives under similar conditions. Start seed indoors in Jiffy-7 peat pellets six to eight weeks before transplanting outside after all danger of frost. Set plants 18 inches apart in rows 30 inches apart, although a 15 ft. row is room enough for 8 plants and plenty to supply a family of four. They grow well in containers, and like a soil with good tilth enriched with well decomposed garden compost, and a packaged vegetable fertilizer.

Black-fruited eggplants are most popular, and in recent years breeders have worked towards creating the best eggplant shape. Contrary to popular belief, the fat round eggplants are not the most practical. Long, slender pear-shaped kinds like *Jersey King* are considered best. All eggplants on the inside are white, but the outer skin can vary in color among varieties. Both white and yellow eggplants exist, and although they are said to taste good they are not popular, and therefore not readily available.

A packet of hybrid eggplant normally contains 30 seeds of reliable germination.

(Left) Jersey King hybrid eggplant is an excellent variety for home gardens.

(Above) This is the shape most American gardeners like to see in an eggplant. In the orient, however, it is the more slender pear-shaped kinds that are more popular.

(Below) White eggplants are not new. This illustration appeared in a seed catalog more than 60 years ago but the variety disappeared through lack of demand.

51

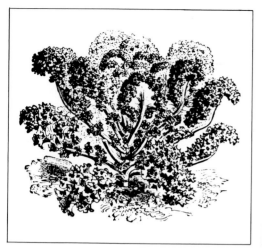

KALE
Hardiest of All

This hardy vegetable green is a valuable fresh winter vegetable, resisting the heat of summer and cold of winter better than any other garden vegetable.

Best grown as a fall crop, seed should be sown outdoors in July to follow a planting of peas, sowing seed 1/4 in. deep, and thinning plants to 12 ins. apart.

Frost improves the flavor of the leaves, and a straw mulch in fall will help them through the winter.

A recommended variety is *Curled Vates*. Cook it like spinach by harvesting leaves from several plants. A packet of seed will normally sow a 30 ft. row, although 15 ft. of Kale in your garden is generally ample.

KOHL-RABI
Flavor Like a Water Chestnut

It seems that Kohl-Rabi would be more popular if more people knew how to cook it, since it is extremely easy to grow in a wide range of soils.

A member of the cabbage family, kohl-rabi forms a thick round bulb above ground where the stem meets the soil. When young, this fleshy bulb has a texture and delicate flavor not unlike water chestnuts.

Kohl-rabi can be cooked whole, sliced thin, diced or chopped into "matchsticks" for adding raw to salad. Added to mixed vegetable soup, it imparts a delicious crisp flavor.

52

Sow seed in early spring four weeks before your last frost date, or in late summer for fall crops. Seed should be planted 1/2 in. deep in rows 1 ft. apart, and thinned to stand 6 in. apart in the row. A packet will normally sow a 40 ft. row, but 15 ft. is plenty.

Recommended variety is *Early White Vienna*, ready to eat after 55 days when the bulbs are 2-1/2 to 3 inches across.

LEEKS
Worth Waiting For

Leeks are another vegetable that deserve to be more widely grown since they can be harvested right up to December. If you have never tasted hot leek soup during winter evenings in front of a roaring log fire you have missed a flavor experience that undoubtedly accounts for this vegetable being the national emblem of Wales.

Leeks need a long growing season, but they are hardy, and germinate reliably during early spring. Growing long and slender, they can be sown thickly and thinned to 2 ins. apart. Some catalogs will recommend 12 ins. spacing, but that's wasteful and entirely unnecessary.

Flavor is not unlike asparagus, but with a delicate onion flavor, and thinnings can be used as scallions. They freeze well, and combine well with cooked potatoes, or added to vegetable soups and stews.

Broad London is a recommended variety, and although it is not essential, leeks can be blanched by heaping loose earth up around the stalks as they mature.

A packet will normally sow a 25 ft. row, but a 15 ft. row will grow up to 90 leeks. Soil needs are similar to onions — they like lots of well decomposed garden compost or manure in addition to a vegetable fertilizer.

(*Above*) *Lettuce Great Lakes is an excellent crisp-head lettuce with the distinction of an All-America award.*

(*Below*) *Okra Clemson Spineless, an All-America winner, is still the finest okra after 30 years since its introduction by the South Carolina Experiment Station.*

(*Above*) *Kale, Scotch Curled is so hardy it will provide fresh greens all through winter in most areas of the United States — especially if given a thick layer of straw mulch.*

(*Top, left*) *Eggplants do well wherever tomatoes and peppers can be grown.*

53

54

(Above) Tri-X Seedless watermelon is considered to be three times sweeter than other kinds, hence its name. Seedless watermelons do produce a few small, immature edible seeds.

(Top) A seedless watermelon growing on the vine. To test for ripeness tap the top with your knuckle. If it sounds like tapping your chest it's ripe. If it sounds like your forehead — it's underripe.

(Top left) Cantaloupe production like this depends on several optimum conditions — but most important are a warm, fertile soil and long sunny periods at time of maturity.

(Left) Burpee Hybrid Cantaloupe has everything — good looks, large size with heavy netting and delicious flavor. Some truck farmers and roadside stands do such a good repeat business with this super-productive melon they often keep its name a secret.

Crisp head lettuce shown at right has a crunchy heart, but takes longer to grow than looseleaf lettuce which is the kind most often grown in home gardens.

(Below) A good way to grow head lettuce is to start them in seedling planters for transplanting into the garden at least 9 inches apart. Looseleaf lettuce will take crowding, but head lettuce may fail to develop heads if it is planted too close together.

LETTUCE
Space-Saving Ideas

This king of salad vegetables loves cool weather, but succession plantings of the right varieties can assure a steady supply from spring until fall.

Looseleaf lettuce is the quickest and easiest to grow, requiring just six weeks from seed to harvest. Head lettuce takes twice as long to reach maturity, but it has that crisp, brittle texture which adds body to salads. If Caesar salad is your favorite then *Cos* lettuce is the variety to grow.

Sow looseleaf lettuce directly into the garden four weeks before your last frost date, or indoors to get leafy transplants.

There's a special reason to grow *Oak Leaf* lettuce. When it's time to harvest you don't have to pull up the entire plant. Instead, you can pick the outer leaves of several plants, and more new leaves will grow to take their place. That way they remain productive for a longer period. *Oak Leaf* is also the most heat resistant lettuce and the earliest (40 days).

Among the heading lettuce, by far the most flavorful and heat resistant is *Buttercrunch* (see page 28 for full description). Two good looseleaf lettuce with ornamental value are *Salad Bowl* (frilly leaves) and *Ruby*, which is tinged red.

Lettuce does not need sowing in single rows spaced 1 1/2 feet apart like so many catalogs recommend. In small gardens that's a terrible waste of space. You will gain much more productivity if you start the seed indoors, then harden off and transplant just six inches apart so they rub shoulders, with *three* lines in a diamond pattern filling a 1 1/2 foot wide row. Sow seed 1/2 in. deep and cover with fine soil.

For lettuce 9 months of the year, construct a cold frame with wooden sides — and keep covered with glass during colder months. This way only the coldest months of January and February will be too severe to produce anything. In a 4 ft. x 2 ft. cold frame you can jam 32 lettuce heads shoulder-to-shoulder.

Lettuce is a favorite target for many kinds of pests — mice, shrews, deer, cut-worms, slugs and others. Vegetable dusts and wood ashes will provide effective controls.

Lettuce is not fussy about soil, although for best results it likes its soil fertile and loose. A packet of seed normally sows a 40 ft. row.

55

(Left) The most popular kind of melon is one heavily ribbed and netted, like this. Feel for ripeness by gently pushing in the stem or blossom end. If it feels slightly soft the melon is ripe.

(Below) Crenshaw melons are the kind sold as expensive dessert melons in gourmet restaurants at $2.00 a slice. It used to be that they could be grown only in Southern California and the Deep South, but this new Early Hybrid Crenshaw can be grown even in northern states as far north as New York, requiring just 80 days to ripen from seed.

MELON
Food of the Gods

Nothing in the vegetable garden can quite match the pride and pleasure you will feel in growing your first big, juicy, sun-ripened, mouth-watering cantaloupes (or muskmelons).

Melon seed is easy-to-handle, germinates rapidly if planted after all danger of frost, and as the vines grow fast during the hot, humid days of summer, you'll find yourself drawn to the garden each evening just to admire the progress of your melon vines.

Melon growing really is very easy, but many beginner gardeners are discouraged because of the space they occupy. What few people seem to realize is that melons will grow happily up trellis, and the heavy ripening melons can be supported by "slings" of cloth to occupy no more space in your garden than tomato plants.

Melons have some definite needs, of course. They like a loose, crumbly, fertile soil enriched with well decomposed manure or compost. Mulching is a big help, since their roots need plenty of moisture and warmth. A black plastic mulch has been found best for melons since it not only keeps the ground warm and moist, but also discourages weeds.

Every seed catalog or seed display will offer a tempting selection of fine melon varieties. *Pride of Wisconsin* is a fine, popular cantaloupe that fresh fruit stands each year do a roaring business with. A dollar and more per melon is what many people will pay to sample its delicious sweet orange flesh, yet a packet will plant dozens of vines — each vine capable of yielding up to a dozen luscious fruit.

Best of the Crenshaw type melons is a beauty called *Early Hybrid Crenshaw*. This variety allows even northern states to grow Crenshaws (see page 32 for full description).

Sow seed of melons 1/2 in. deep after all danger of frost in groups or "hills," thinning seedlings to one sturdy plant in each group. Allow six feet between each group if you leave the vines to sprawl on the ground — or three groups to a 15 ft. row. A packet of hybrid seed is sufficient to sow 12 hills in the open, or 50 plants started indoors in Jiffy-7 peat pellets for transplanting.

56

MUSHROOMS
If You Like a Challenge

I had a friend who loved fresh mushrooms so much he wanted to grow his own. He bought all the right materials, made his own indoor mushroom beds, and did everything "just the way the experts said." After nine months of waiting and no sign of mushrooms he finally gave up in disgust, tore down his mushroom beds and emptied the soil outside at the back of his tool shed. The next morning he could hardly believe his eyes — there in the thousands were the plump white mushrooms.

There's probably nothing more challenging in the world of gardening than growing your own mushrooms from mushroom spawn. Given the right conditions, they can be grown year round in a shed, outhouse, cellar, barn or coldframe — in fact any place in darkness where temperatures will not fall to below 50°.

Mushrooms are an edible fungus, and reproduce themselves by spores which form in the gills on the underside of the mushroom. If you place a mature mushroom on a piece of white paper away from draughts you will soon see the paper covered with a fine brown "dust" — the reproductive spores. Under ideal conditions these brown spores will produce white threads like a spider's web. Again, under ideal conditions, these white threads (called mycelium or mushroom spawn) will grow mushrooms. Mushroom spawn you buy to grow mushrooms indoors is mycelium that has been allowed to grow, then arrested in its growth by drying. Growth is renewed by providing favorable conditions again.

Fresh stable manure is the most reliable growing medium for mushrooms. The stable manure should be heaped, left to ferment, and the heap turned and watered down every three days for four weeks until the manure is dark brown with no offensive smell. Your mushroom bed can then be made up from this.

Deep boxes are ideal for holding the manure, which should be spread out to 9 inches deep. The ideal temperature for a spawning bed is 70° F., and the bed should be neither too dry nor too wet. A good test is to squeeze the manure in your hand. If you can squeeze water out of it, then it's too wet.

There are different kinds of spawn available. Usually it comes as a "cake" to be broken up into lumps and planted like bulbs. Spawn also comes in granular form to be sown like seeds, then covered with manure.

After planting, the spawn should soon begin to produce thousands of white threads and spread all over the bed. After about two weeks the beds should be covered with a layer of clean garden soil about 1 inch thick and firmed down with the back of a spade. This is called "casing". The ideal temperature at this time is 60° F. Keep the bed moist by an overhead spray, and watch for mushrooms about six to eight weeks from spawning. They should be picked regularly by twisting the stem from the bed.

Be careful when buying pre-planted "Mushroom kits". Even with the best of them they normally won't produce more than a handful of mushrooms — hardly enough for a good breakfast.

Growing your own mushrooms is certainly a lot of trouble, but once you succeed you'll feel prouder than a new parent.

OKRA
Fruitful and Decorative

Although Okra is noted as a Southern vegetable, it can be grown reliably as far north as New York State. Related to hibiscus, it produces white hibiscus-type flowers on tall stalks. As the flower fades, a young pod starts to grow from the base. These pods should be collected while young and cooked or added to soups and stews. In India and the Middle East they are an essential ingredient in meat curries. Pods left on the plant for more than a few days soon become tough and stringy, but left to fully mature and dry out in fall, they are extremely decorative and prized for dried flower arrangements.

For worthwhile results you will need three 15 ft. rows, and in this respect Okra is not recommended for the small garden.

After soaking in warm water for 24 hours, plant seed 1/2 in. deep in rows 2 1/2 ft. apart, thinning the seedlings to 15 in apart. Well rotted manure or garden compost worked into the soil will produce best results, in addition to a commercial vegetable fertilizer.

Recommended variety: *Clemson Spineless* (All-America Winner).

PARSLEY

Parsley is king of herbs and high in nutritional value. Use as a garnish on meats, salads, egg dishes, soups, sandwiches, fish and potatoes.

Always soak the seed for 24 hours in warm water before sowing into the garden — otherwise it can be one of the slowest of garden seeds to germinate. Apart from this requirement there is little else to know about growing parsley. It seems to thrive under a wide range of soil and climate conditions.

Mature plants are extremely hardy, and in most areas plants will stay productive into December. If a straw mulch is applied for protection after that it will yield even into the following spring before going to seed.

Make one sowing in April for summer crops (parsley is frost-hardy) and another in July to obtain young plants for transplanting to pots for growing indoors in a sunny window. Sow seed in rows 1/2 inch deep, 1 ft. wide, and thin seedlings to six inches apart. A packet of seed normally plants a 30 ft row.

Parsley is at home in a flower bed, especially as a decorative edging. Plain and curly-leafed varieties are sold, but the curly leaf kind is by far the most popular.

Planted in a wire basket, it can make a magnificent hanging plant — but it must always have full sun. It cannot tolerate shade.

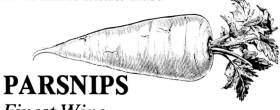

PARSNIPS
Finest Wine

Although similar to carrots in shape, parsnips need twice the growing time (about 4 months) to mature their creamy white roots. In England parsnips are not only prized as a cooked vegetable, they make the finest of all vegetable wines. Also they store well and can remain in the garden until the ground freezes. Left too long in the ground they become tough and woody.

Sow seed at the same time as carrots — four weeks before your last frost date — in deeply spaded soil of good tilth 1/2 in. deep in rows 2 ft. apart, thinning seedlings to 4 in. apart. One 15 ft. row will produce 45 parsnips — plenty for fresh use and storing. Recommended variety : *All-American*

PEANUTS
Grows Like Clover, Tastes Like a Nut

Related to beans, peanuts can be grown successfully over most of the United States wherever corn is grown. Peanuts for planting come in their shells, and although they can be planted in the shell, it is best to remove them since this will double your seed supply.

Plant seeds two inches apart after danger of frost, and later thin to 1 ft. apart in rows 2 ft. apart.

The most interesting aspect of peanuts is the way they form the nuts. The plants grow like clumps of clover and produce yellow "pea-shaped" flowers. When fertilized they send out a probe which digs into the ground and creates the peanuts.

A packet will normally sow a 50 ft. row, and a minimum of 15 plants in a 15 ft. row is essential for worthwhile production. Needs a long growing season (100 days).

RHUBARB *Pie Plant*

There's space in every garden for a clump or two of tasty rhubarb. The thick, deliciously-flavored stems make scrumptious pies. Stewed as a fruit dessert, there is nothing among the fresh fruits to equal it in early spring.

A hardy perennial, rhubarb is easily grown from roots or seeds planted in spring. An excellent variety to try is *Valentine* with deep red stalks and succulent sweet flavor.

Planted in spring in fertile soil, roots will ensure a good crop the following spring, while seeds may take an extra year to reach good size. Space roots 3 ft. apart with crowns just below the surface, and remove any flower stalks which appear since these will rob the roots of energy. For the most part, rhubarb is a carefree plant, but it does demand a deeply cultivated, richly organic soil to give its best. It thrives on plenty of compost or well-rotted manure.

Well-established rhubarb roots can be forced into earlier production by placing a bottomless bucket or peach basket over the crowns in late February. The protected growing tips will then seek the light, growing tall more quickly than if left in the open. One final word of caution — never eat rhubarb leaves. In spite of the stems being good to eat and rich in vitamins, the leaves themselves contain a poison, and should be discarded.

SALSIFY *Oyster Plant*

When I first read that salsify tastes like oysters I scoffed at the thought, and decided it was a seedsman's wild imagination. When I finally got around to tasting salsify I was surprised to discover that the taste *did* remind me of oysters. But even if you don't like oysters you might like salsify since the texture and mild flavor are delicious.

Growing long, tapering roots crowned with sword-like leaves, salsify needs a deeply spaded soil of good tilth, and a long growing season (about five months). Sow seed four weeks before last frost date in rows 1/2 in.

deep. thinning seedlings to 3 in. apart. A 15 ft. row will produce 60 roots. Salsify can stay in the ground until the ground freezes, or it can be stored in a box of sand in a cool basement.

Recommended variety *Mammoth Sandwich Island*.

SPINACH *Rich in Vitamins*

Spinach is a valuable vegetable for small gardens because it can be planted early and harvested before much else in the garden is ready for picking. Spinach salad is even better than a lettuce-based salad.

Sow seeds six weeks before the last frost date in soil with a good tilth (light, rich, moist and finely worked). A mulch to conserve moisture in the soil is recommended. Plant seeds 1/2 inch deep in rows, spacing seedlings to six inches apart. A 15 ft. row will produce 30 plants, but greater productivity in a small garden can be obtained by planting two rows shoulder to shoulder, to make a 1 1/2 ft. broad row, since a single packet will plant up to 30 ft. of spinach. Allow 18 ins. of room in a diamond pattern on either side between the next vegetable rows.

Dusting with wood ashes or vegetable dust will deter most insect pests. Recommended variety is *America*, an All-America award winner.

Spinach demands cool growing conditions. In addition to early spring, late summer is another recommended sowing time so plants mature in fall.

SUNFLOWER

The sunflower has become a symbol of self-sufficient living. In Russia they are a vital part of the economy producing food for poultry and humans, and also providing oil for fuel and light.

The object of growing sunflowers is to create as big a head as possible. *Mammoth Russian* is the variety to grow, and the large striped seeds should be sown after the last frost date in a fertile soil preferably enriched with compost or well decomposed manure, and a vegetable fertilizer.

Mature heads will attract colorful seed-eating birds to your garden, and the seeds are good to eat.

A packet normally contains 100 seeds, but for small gardens two or three plants are plenty.

ONIONS *Organic Lovers*

Onions are an essential flavor enhancer for so many meals in both salads and main dishes, chopped, sliced, fried or braised. Stuffed onions are a gourmet delight, and they combine well with potatoes, tomatoes and hamburger.

The most important requirement for good onions is a well-drained soil, heavily enriched with well rotted manure or compost. Even a soil rich in fertilizer will grow only half the weight of onions without well decomposed manure, according to the National Vegetable Research Station, in England.

Two types of onions are worth growing - the spring or bunching onions and the large bulbous kinds. Bunching onions are best grown from seed, and although the large bulbing onions will grow readily from seed, quicker results can be expected from onion sets.

The accepted way of sowing seeds is to plant them 1/2 in. deep in rows spaced 9 to 12 inches apart. A packet of the small black seeds will normally plant a 30 ft. row, trickled as thinly and evenly as possible, then thinned later to 6 inches apart. In small gardens, however, heavier yields are possible by closing up the rows 4 to 5 inches apart.

Onion seed should be planted as early in the spring as possible, six weeks before the last frost date, and they cannot tolerate weeds. Generally, the earlier you sow, the heavier the crop. The seedlings are extremely hardy and frost will not harm them.

When planting onion sets, space the sets 1 inch apart and pull every other one for early spring scallions, leaving the others to mature into regular-size onions for late summer and fall harvest.

Yellow Sweet Spanish and *Southport Yellow Globe* are two reliable old-established varieties, although several new hybrids are worth trying. Red and white varieties are also available.

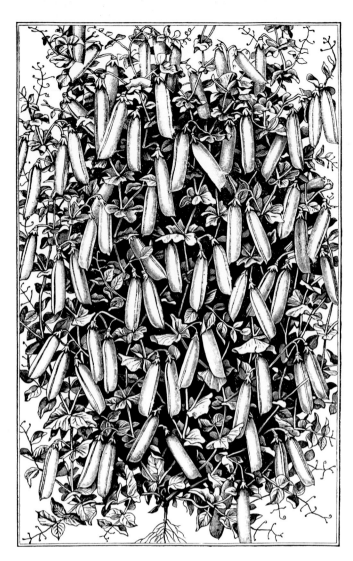

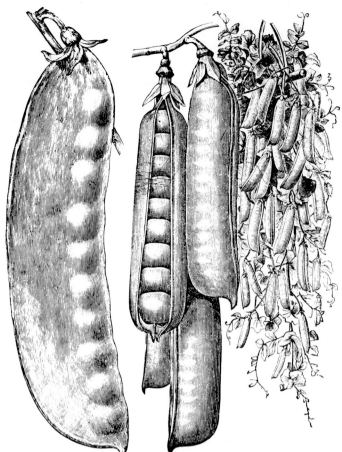

(Left) For perfect pea pods filled to the tip like these, days must be cool, the soil must be fertile, and watering should be done twice a week in the absence of a drenching rain.

(Right) Edible podded peas must be picked before the seeds start to swell in the pod, since the skin soon takes on a tough, stringy texture.

GARDEN PEAS
More to the Pod

Peas are one of the earliest crops to plant in the spring. As soon as the soil is dry after the winter freeze is time to plant. The seedlings tolerate frost and will make quick growth to mature before hot weather.

Two kinds of peas are best to grow in American gardens - the regular garden peas, which you must shell, and the sugar pod peas, which you eat pod and all. With both types of peas there are tall and dwarf varieties. The advantage of dwarf varieties is that you don't have the extra work of putting up poles or trellis to support the vines.

In addition to a spring planting, peas can be sown again in midsummer to have a second crop during the cool weather of fall. They need good sunlight and a fertile soil with a good tilth since the roots like to go deep, but apart from that they look after themselves. Peas generally take up rather a lot of space for the yields they give, but the new variety *Green Arrow* is worth some space in the small garden since it bears more peas

to the pod (see page 29 for full description). *Lincoln*, which has a reputation for being the best flavored of all garden peas, is also a recommended variety. Plant peas 1 in. deep and 2 ins. apart in rows 24 ins. apart. A well-grown 15 ft. row will produce up to 12 lbs. of shelled peas.

The sugar pod peas are especially good to grow, as it is these which the Chinese use extensively in their cooking. The pods need picking young before the peas swell the pod. In addition to being delicious, they are also labor-saving since there's no shelling involved. Just pop them in the pot with water and cook for 15 minutes. Dwarf Grey Sugar is a real labor-saving variety - no shelling and no poles for support. What more can you ask of a vegetable?

When peas stop bearing at the onset of hot days, remove the vines and plant in their place a row of broccoli, cauliflower or Brussels sprouts to mature in fall.

(*Above*) Peanuts grow under the soil at the end of strings which protrude from yellow pea-shaped flowers.

(*Right*) Rhubarb Valentine needs plenty of room, but one healthy clump like this is often sufficient to supply a family of four rhubarb lovers.

(*Above*) Spinach America needs just 50 days to mature from seed, providing the entire growing period takes place during cool weather of spring or fall.

(*Left*) Pepper Long Red Cayenne is a hot variety often known as "chili peppers". Dried and hung from strings they are extremely decorative.

(Top) Potato Katahdin, a superior heavy yielding variety.

(Bottom, left) This photo proves there are many kinds of radish other than red. Featured here are white and bi-colored varieties.

(Bottom, right) White icicle radish grows long tapering roots, best eaten before they reach five inches in length.

62

Peppers and tomatoes are closely related. To get good size fruit ripening early, a fertilizer high in phosphorus is necessary.

PEPPERS
Easy to Start Your Own

Large-fruited bell peppers have the mildest, sweetest flavor, while the small-fruited kinds are hot and pungent. Pepper seed, like tomato seed, is long-lived and germinates reliably. So starting your own plants from seed indoors is a good practice, with the object of growing healthy foot-high transplants for setting out into your garden after all danger of frost. Allow six to eight weeks from seed to transplanting, starting the seeds in peat pellets or seedling planters, setting out plants 24 inches apart with 30 inches between rows.

The bushy, compact plants occupy very little space for the yields they give, and for this reason they are ideal subjects for containers, serving as both fruitful and ornamental plants. A sunny location is necessary, plus a fertile soil. Failure of fruit to ripen is generally due to too much nitrogen and insufficient phosphorus, and an application of vegetable fertilizer high in phosphorus will normally do the trick. *One 15 ft. row with seven or eight plants is ample for a family of four,* and a packet of hybrid pepper seed is normally sufficient to grow a minimum of 50 plants.

When harvesting it is best to use a sharp knife or pruning scissors to separate fruit from the plant, since the branches are brittle and may break if pulled.

Bell peppers are the most widely grown kinds, and these ripen from green to red, but don't let them stay red too long as they soon deteriorate after ripening. Golden yellow bell peppers are also available, and one of the most decorative ideas for a kitchen is to dry red and yellow peppers to hang in bunches.

Best of the bell peppers is the All-America winner *Bell Boy* (see full description page 33), while *Golden Calwonder* is a good yellow variety. *Red Chili* and *Long Red Cayenne* are hot, prolific and decorative. In a class all its own is *Sweet Banana*, an All-America winner, growing pineapple-yellow fruit which ripen red.

One of the best uses of bell peppers is stuffed with spicy hamburger or meatballs and served with stewed tomatoes.

Question: I have tried some hybrid kinds of peppers and don't see much difference in yields from the standard varieties. Why not?

Answer: Your garden is lacking either sunlight, moisture or plant nutrients. Probably plant nutrients. Use a vegetable garden fertilizer high in phosphorus. Given this extra energy you should see the hybrid pepper plants double the yields of standard varieties given the same treatment. Same with any other hybrid.

63

POTATO
Pioneer Food

Ever seen potato-tomato plants advertised? It's a swindle. What you'll get is a potato with a tomato plant in the middle. They sprout together, and since they look so much alike in appearance you can hardly tell the two apart. The roots of the potato below ground produce potatoes while the stems of the tomato above ground produce fruit. Not an ideal way of growing either, but to some degree it will work.

Root crops such as potatoes are the most under-rated vegetables. When gardeners think of mouth-watering exotic vegetables it's cantaloupes and watermelons that spring quickly to mind. Yet these are seasonal tastes you would soon get tired of if you had to eat them every day. You can't say the same for potatoes. For some reason root crops like potatoes are more of a food staple for man than other kinds of vegetables.

Potatoes do require a lot of room, but what a thrill it is to eat new potatoes with melted butter, dug fresh from the soil within hours of cooking.

Soil for potatoes must be deeply dug and fertile, and seed potatoes should be bought. Actually, any supermarket potato can be used by cutting out around the green sprouts and planting. However, I prefer to plant named varieites — and *Katahdin* is my favorite, although a late variety.

Plant the seed potatoes in early spring, cutting each seed potato into slices with an eye in each slice. Each eye should face up planted 4 inches deep, 18 inches apart in rows 24 inches apart. When the sprouts have grown about six inches high start piling loose soil around them or a mulch of straw or peat. The stems will create more roots and grow heavier yields of potatoes.

After the stems have died down in late summer the potatoes will be ready for harvesting. They store well over winter in a dry cool basement.

Sweet potatoes require soils with an especially fine tilth for best results. One sweet potato tuber will produce dozens of sprouts, each one capable of producing a healthy full-size plant. The best way to do this is to lay the tuber in a dish of moist sand indoors. Soon sprouts with roots will form all along the sides and with a sharp knife you can cut out a chunk of sweet potato with sprout and root, then plant it. Four months of warm weather are needed for reliable sweet potatoes.

Normal production from a potato plant is 10 potatoes averaging 10 pounds in weight. Heaping straw or shredded leaves around the stems will encourage extra roots and potatoes that can be harvested without digging for them.

64

PUMPKIN
How to Grow a Giant Pumpkin

There's something about a pumpkin that makes people happy, and the bigger the pumpkins the happier they seem to make people feel — especially children. Very few garden accomplishments can match the enjoyment and sense of achievement experienced in growing your very own pumpkin from seed.

Giant pumpkin growing contests are probably more popular today than beauty contests, and the world record stands at 399 lbs.

The most important consideration in growing a giant pumpkin is to choose the right variety. The *Jack O'Lantern* is fine for Halloween displays, and the *Sugar* or *New England* pumpkins are the best for making pies, but to grow a really BIG specimen that will be the envy of your neighborhood, the best variety of all is called *Big Max*, available from most color packet displays and seed catalogs.

Big Max will grow to 200 lbs. weight — and more — if you know a few simple pumpkin-growing secrets.

First a good fertile soil is essential, especially if it is enriched with compost or well decomposed manure or a commercial vegetable fertilizer. Second, it must have a sunny location. Third, it must be kept watered — particularly during dry spells — since it is moisture absorption which increases the pumpkin's weight. Fourth, never allow more than one pumpkin to grow on each vine. This way all the plant's energy is concentrated into making one extra-large fruit.

It's interesting to see a pumpkin grow. The large, easy-to-handle seeds are best planted after danger of frost, to a depth of 1 inch in groups or "hills" spaced 6 ft. apart. Plant six seeds to each hill and thin to two healthy vines. A packet will plant 5 groups. Within 10 days two large first-leaves will thrust through the soil. Daily you will be able to see the young plant make fast growth, creating a lush vine with two kinds of colorful yellow flowers — males and females. You can tell the female flowers because they have miniature pumpkins ready to be fertilized by pollen from the males.

The only space saving idea with pumpkins is to plant a new bush variety called *"Cinderella"* producing 10 in. fruits on plants that resemble summer squash and require 3 ft. by 3 ft. of space. Two plants are ample for a small garden.

Pumpkins originated in America, and pumpkin pie was first served to the Pilgrim Fathers at their first Thanksgiving dinner of roast wild turkey and cranberry sauce. It's certainly a wonderful vegetable — what else has the gift of being good to eat, decorative to look at, fun to grow and the power to make people happy?

Since pumpkin seeds are good to eat, but require a lot of tedious shelling, breeders are now developing "naked seeded" pumpkins, although presently they are not the decorative kind. An edible, decorative, naked-seeded pumpkin is on the list of objectives among top pumpkin breeders.

PUMPKIN HIDEAWAY

A good way to get children interested in gardening — and keep them out of mischief — is to help them build a hideout camouflaged with pumpkin vines, melons or gourds.

All that's needed is a 5 ft. square frame covered along the top and three sides by chicken wire. Dig a strip of ground along two sides and cultivate to a depth of at least 1½ ft., adding compost and a little fertilizer.

Plant seeds of pumpkin, melon or gourds about 12 inches apart along both sides in late May and water regularly. The seeds will soon sprout and grow rapidly, climbing up the chicken wire. Soon it will be completely covered with dense vines, and the children will have great fun in their hidden playhouse.

Within a few weeks of sprouting the vines will begin to bear lovely flowers and then form fruit. Melons for eating; pumpkins for Jack 'O Lanterns and gourds for drying to make decorations. Cucumbers and vine squash are also good to use.

Edward Gancarz (Top right), a champion pumpkin grower living in New Jersey, exhibits a 312 lb. pumpkin with which he won the Newtown (Pennsylvania) pumpkin growing contest. It's enough to make more than 300 pies.

The young lady below has a lot to smile about in a patch of Big Max pumpkins being grown from seed. Big Max is the biggest pumpkin available in general commerce, and will grow to more than 150 lbs. with adequate moisture and fertilizer.

PUMPKIN FACTS

RELATED TO: cucumbers. Ornamental gourds and squash are also members of the same family (cucurbits).

USES: Pies, soup, bread. Seeds edible, shelled like sunflower seeds.

PUMPKIN CONTESTS: There is a fierce rivalry among dedicated pumpkin growers. Sabotage is common. Growers often have to hide their pumpkin patches. One group of New Jersey growers reported they were spied on by a rival with a helicopter.

FEEDING: Pumpkins increase their weight by moisture absorption, and to grow really big will require the equivalent of 8 inches of rainfall per week to grow 7 to 10 lbs. **per day.** Fertilizer high in nitrogen is best. Overfeeding, however, will cause the pumpkin to burst.

Milk feeding or beer feeding is an old trick whereby a wool wick enclosed in a plastic tube to prevent evaporation is inserted into the pumpkin stem from a gallon jug of milk or beer.

PUMPKIN CARVING: It's possible to carve your name on the skin when the pumpkin is small and still growing, by scratching the skin with a sharp point. The scratch will then form a scab and as the pumpkin grows so will your name.

POLLINATION: Pumpkins have two kinds of flowers — male and female. The males come first, followed by the females, and in order to get an early fruit set it's necessary to keep a watchful eye for that first female. You can tell them because they have a baby pumpkin already formed under the flower. Take a camel's hair brush and transfer some pollen from the center of the male flower to the center of the female in the early morning. If this is not done the baby pumpkin may shrivel up and die. In nature pumpkin flowers are pollinated by insects, but when you want to win a giant pumpkin contest and get an early fruit set, it's more reliable to do it by hand.

OTHER ADVICE: To grow a giant pumpkin, choose a variety capable of growing big like **Big Max.** Plant seeds directly into the soil. To begin with let a lot of fruit set, then when they're the size of a grapefruit examine them carefully for shape, color and most important — a thick growing stem. Then pick off all the other pumpkins leaving the best one to receive all the attention. Pick off all female flowers as they form, and don't let the vine form roots close to the stem, otherwise it could pull the stem right out of the pumpkin as it grows.

66

Pumpkins galore are a familiar sight in fall at roadside stands and garden centers throughout America, a fitting symbol of America's fruitfulness.

68

Strawberry Jersey Belle, grown to perfection on fertile soil that has been mulched with straw to keep fruit clean.

STRAWBERRY

Grow Your Own

Among the most rewarding crops you could ever grow are strawberries. Store-bought strawberries are never cheap, and it's so easy to grow your own — even in a window box or an old barrel. Just a few simple rules have to be followed to ensure success.

An extra-fertile soil is essential. The main object with strawberries is to grow bushy plants with as many leaves as possible since the flower buds which later form the fruit are produced in the leaf axils. Therefore, the more leafy your strawberry plants the more fruitful they will be.

Young plants (certified virus-free) can be bought from local nurseries or through the mail. Select those with long fibrous roots and healthy dark green leaves. Leaves showing red spots are diseased. Plant in fertile soil so the growing tip sits snuggly on the surface without being covered over.

Ruthless though it may seem, you should pinch off all flower buds the first year to prevent them from bearing fruit. Also cut off any runners that may develop. By doing this the first year all the energy is directed into growing a strong sturdy plant capable of yielding large quantities of luscious fruit. Plants otherwise may bear only sparse small berries. Fall planting is also recommended.

Keep your strawberry bed weed-free and mulch around the plants to keep the berries from contact with the soil.

If you don't have much room for a strawberry bed there are several worthwhile alternatives. For patios and sun porches buy a strawberry pot. Standing tall and shaped like an urn, it has "pockets" for the plants to grow around the sides. This is the same idea as a "strawberry barrel". You take an old barrel and drill rows of holes in the sides 2 to 3 inches wide. Make drainage holes in the bottom and line with drainage material such as crocks and broken brick. Build up a central core with a perforated pipe or column of tins punctured with holes and filled with loose stones for easy watering. Fill the barrel with good soil and plant strawberries in the holes and around the rim. Place the barrel on bricks and water regularly through the central core.

Another space-saver is a "pyramid garden". Three circular tiers form a "garden-in-the-round" with space for 50 strawberry plants in just 6 ft. of space. It's also available with a sprinkler device, and a frame for covering with anti-bird netting and anti-frost cover.

Alpine Strawberry

One of my most vivid memories during a visit to Spain was walking into a sidewalk cafe in Puerto Pollensa, Majorca, and seeing a teenage couple dig into dessert bowls heaped with wild alpine strawberries, and a swirl of fresh cream on top. Those ripe red berries were so luscious and sweet they needed no sugar and it is my contention that no other berry fruit in the world can match the wild strawberry for flavor.

There is a variety of alpine strawberry which is worth growing in your vegetable garden or flower beds to capture that same flavor. Listed in seed catalogs as *Baron Solemacher* Alpine Strawberry, it grows berries that are twice the size of the wild kind, and since it does not set runners, it stays neat and compact, bearing year after year. Another advantage of *Baron Solemacher* is that you can expect to pick fruit the first year from planting seed by sowing indoors in March, and transplanting seedlings to the garden. Fruit will form in August and September and continue cropping each year at regular strawberry-picking time on neat, compact, bushy plants.

Seed germination of alpine strawberries is erratic, and they need light to germinate, so just press the seeds into your seed starting soil so they sit snuggly in the soil, but are not covered over.

69

RADISH
For Quick Results

One of the quickest vegetables to grow in your garden is radish, second only to cress. Many varieties take less than 30 days to reach good size from seed, and they can be planted straight into the garden four weeks before your last frost date.

For best results radish must be encouraged to grow quickly during the cool conditions of spring in a loose fertile soil. They also need plenty of water during dry spells.

Not all radish are round and red. Some are white, some are half-and-half, and others are shaped like icicles with long tapering roots. It's all a matter of taste as to which to choose for your own garden. Most people prefer to use them raw in salads, but an interesting variation is to steam them in thick slices for 10 minutes and serve with butter. The steaming gives them a milder taste, but they stay crisp and delicious.

Left in the garden, radishes will reach an enormous size, but then they become pithy and unusable. Recommended varieties are *Cherry Belle,* an All-America award winner, and *Icicle,* a good white radish.

When planting radish it is best not to sow the entire packet in one go, but to make sowings at regular intervals until the weather turns too hot. Radishes also make a good fall crop. Sow seeds 1/2 in. deep, and thin them to 1 inch apart when they are still small. When planted in straight lines, leave 12 inches between rows. A packet will normally plant a 30 ft. row, although for small gardens two 15 ft. rows sown 4 in. apart is practical.

(Below) Red radish, Cherry Belle, an All-America winner, is extra early and retains its crispness over a long period compared to many other radish varieties.

(Above) Radish roots should not be allowed to grow larger than shown here, since they can become hollow and pithy.

Given cool conditions and adequate moisture at the slightest hint of a dry spell, cherry-size radish can be gathered in 20 days of sowing the seed.

70

Squash Quiz

Try to guess the names of these squash before looking at the key to captions printed below. Summer squash mature early, while Winter squash mature late and have good keeping qualities.

A   B   C

D   E   F

G   H   I

A—Blue Hubbard Squash   C—Buttercup (Winter)   F—Yellow Patti-Pan (Summer)   H—Yellow Crookneck (Summer)
     Boston (Winter types)   D—Striped Cushaw (Winter)   G—White Patti-Pan or Scallop   I—Zucchini Squash (Summer)
B—Butternut (Winter)   E—Gold Nugget (Summer)   (Summer)

Key to squash pictures

Turk's Turban Squash add brilliant color to a fall garden center display, symbol of Thanksgiving. Other squash shown in the picture are Blue Hubbard (grey), True Hubbard (black), Boston (orange-red) and Sugar pumpkins. Apples shown in rear are Winesaps and McIntosh.

SQUASH
The Fun Vegetables

Squash is one of the easiest families of vegetables to grow in your garden — and what fun they are to grow, too.

Native to the American continent, squash were a food staple of the Indians, and in Europe today most families have never even seen a squash, much less tasted one.

Squash flowers are extremely decorative, and they are delicious to eat picked in the early morning and fried in a batter to have with breakfast eggs.

Squash are very easy to grow. The seeds are large and easy to handle — like pumpkin seeds. Also, they like to be sown directly into the garden after danger of frost. They germinate quickly — usually within 10 days — and they grow with ease.

Squash come in many different shapes and sizes, but they are all divided into two distinct groups — summer and winter squash. The summer squash grow quickly, have softer fruit and should be eaten as soon as they are picked. In fact, the more you pick the more fruit will keep growing. Zucchini, patti pans, crooknecks and straightnecks are all examples of summer squash. These all grow on bush type plants and are less demanding of space than the winter squash which are mostly vining.

St. Pat Scallop, a patti-pan squash, is extra productive, and the white fruits are best eaten small (2 in. across). The more you pick them, the more will grow to take their place.

Winter squash have hard outer skins, they take longer to grow, and the fruit can be stored for long periods for eating during late fall and winter. Butternut, hubbard, acorn and buttercup are examples of winter squash. Best varieties for small gardens are the bush acorn squash, particularly an All-America winner called *Table King* which grows the largest size of all the bush acorn squash varieties.

Don't be fooled by the outer appearance of some squash. Many are a dark unappetizing green, but the interiors are golden yellow and full of delicious flavor. Others like the crooknecks are warted and misshapen — but again the creamy yellow interior when cooked and served with butter is a gourmet's delight.

Plant seeds 1/2 in. deep directly into the garden after all danger of frost in groups or "hills" spaced 3 ft. apart and enriched with fertilizer. Thin to one strong healthy plant in each group. A packet will normally plant 8 groups.

73

(Above) Bush acorn squash, Table King is a recent All-America winner growing full-size fruit on bushy, compact plants with extra-small seed cavities.

(Top) Despite its warted appearance, Yellow Crookneck squash are delicious to eat when young and creamy, growing on bush plants.

(*Above*) *Yellow pear tomatoes are excellent for salads, and make a good cocktail snack.*

(*Right*) *Large-fruited hybrid red varieties of tomatoes are the most widely grown in home gardens.*

TOMATOES
How to Grow Them Earlier

When tomatoes were first found growing by European explorers in South America, they imagined the fruit to be poisonous because of its striking resemblance to deadly nightshade, a poisonous plant common throughout Europe. But once this belief was proved wrong, tomatoes rapidly gained favor, and both English and French seedsmen even called them "Love Apples" to help overcome the poison myth.

Few gardening pleasures can match the enjoyment of being the first on the block to pick ripe tomatoes, and there's many a good gardener who feels he's a miserable failure if he doesn't pick his first sun-ripened tomato by July 4th.

Choosing the right varieties is important, since tomatoes are generally classified as early, midseason or late. When buying seed, read the color packet or the catalog description to see how many days are required to reach maturity. An early variety will average 60 days from setting out foot-high plants - and that means starting the seed indoors another 45 days ahead of transplanting to get the required size plants - preferably with flowers already blooming. Start the seed in Jiffy-7 peat pellets, sowing seed 1/2 in. deep. To get good flower and fruit set indoors, however, you should transfer them when they are a foot high to 6 in. pots and shake the flowers to ensure pollination. A packet of hybrid tomato seeds normally contains 50 seeds.

Tomatoes come in many shapes and sizes - some pear shaped, others orange and yellow colored, some the size of cherries, but those that fall into the giant red category - such as *Beefsteak, Big Boy, Rutgers, Early Giant* and *Delicious* are the most universally grown and the most practical for small gardens. For growing in

74

containers choose *Small Fry Hybrid* or *Pixie Hybrid*.

Of course, tomatoes are sensitive to frost, and they should not be put into the garden until danger of frost is over, but if you're tempted to risk an earlier start, peach baskets will afford some protection from cold nights.

Hybrids will also give you a better chance of reaching that early-ripening date, since they have stronger vigor and greater productivity.

Another booster is to use black plastic as mulch. It keeps the soil warm, maintains an even soil temperature. It also conserves water and keeps down weeds. Once you've tried black plastic you'll never raise tomatoes without it.

A fertile soil is another must, and a vegetable fertilizer high in phosphorus to ensure early fruit ripening should be applied at least twice during the growing season - when the plants are first set outside; and when the fruit has started to form.

For best quality fruit free from sunscald, cracking and ground rot, try growing your tomatoes on stakes. This way you can space the plants two feet apart. If you don't have time for staking you should mulch between the plants since mulching will help keep the fruit clean and reduce rotting, in addition to moisture conservation and weed control.

Disease-resistant tomatoes are also more likely to produce early results, and these are identified by the initials, VF meaning verticillium and fusarium wilt resistant, the most common tomato diseases.

Follow these guidelines, and there's a good chance you will be the first on your block to pick ripe fruit.

Tomato Spring Giant is everything you could wish for in a large-fruited tomato. An All-America winner, it is early, extra productive, disease-resistant and the fruits are perfectly round with excellent flavor.

Commerical tomato production under glass is becoming increasingly popular as a cash crop in the northern and mid-western states. Here tomato plants are growing on bales of hay dressed with fertilizer and living proof that the secret of good growth is sunlight, moisture and plant nutrients. Even soil is not essential.

SEE LEFT PAGE

(Top) Tomato production peaks in August, and at this time it's possible to buy bushel baskets full of local-grown sun-ripened fruit at bargain prices for canning and freezing, as this garden center display testifies.

(Bottom, center) It's all a matter of personal taste whether you like yellow-fruited tomatoes. They are more popular in rural areas, particularly among farming families.

(Bottom, left) These cherry tomatoes, called Small Fry, won an All-America award for their extraordinary heavy yields. They grow well in pots supported by a stake, and are even used as hanging baskets.

Pear tomatoes (bottom, right) are used extensively for making tomato paste. This variety, called Roma is considered to be the best.

If you've been put off eating turnips because of the strong flavor, try the new hybrid white varieties which are best harvested when the size of a golf ball. They are so sweet and juicy at this stage it's hard to believe they are a turnip.

TURNIPS

Sensational New Hybrids Purple-top turnips are colorful, and flower arrangers often use them for table settings featuring other colorful vegetables.

For best quality, turnips must be allowed to make quick growth during cool weather of spring or fall.

Plants are hardy, and seed may be sown early in spring four weeks before the last frost date. The tops are edible and the roots may be stored over winter in a box of sand in a cool basement. In fall, a mulch of straw or chopped leaves will allow them to be harvested into January. Frost improves the flavor of foliage.

In any listing of turnips, a variety called *Tokyo Cross* is earliest of all - up to 15 days earlier than other varieties (see page 29 for full description).

Another recommended variety is *Just Right Hybrid*, giving good flavor in both the white roots and the green foliage. Tops can be harvested within 30 days of seeding.

The accepted planting method is to sow seed 1/4 in. deep in rows 18 in. apart, thinning seedlings to stand six inches apart. However, in small gardens to conserve space it's possible to close-up spacing to 4 inches apart, gaining 45 turnips to a 15 ft. row. A packet of seed will normally sow a 50 ft. row.

A loose, fertile soil will yield best.

(Below) Turnips are a favorite food of the Ford family, yielding leafy edible green tops and flavorful roots as a featured vegetable at many a White House dinner.

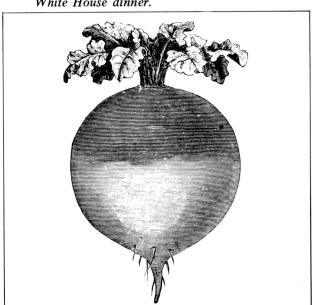

The large oblong watermelons like these are no longer popular with home gardeners. The small, round "ice-box" types are not only earlier and easier to grow, they are more practical as a family food.

WATERMELONS
Red, Yellow and Seedless

Watermelons are not normally associated with small gardens, but to save space they can be grown up trellis like cucumbers, and as the watermelon fruits mature their weight can be supported by slings made from nylon stockings or cloth. This is how many vegetable breeders grow them under controlled greenhouse conditions in winter, and the system works equally well outdoors in summer.

Like cucumbers, watermelons are best planted in groups where a hole has been dug to enrich the soil with manure, compost or fertilizer, planting seed 1 inch deep after all danger of frost, six seeds to a group, finally thinning them down to two strong healthy plants. A packet of seed is normally sufficient to grow 50 plants — or 8 hills, although some of the hybrids contain less (about 10 seeds).

On page 28 we describe the benefits of the seedless watermelons, and the new yellow watermelon, *Yellow Baby*, which belongs to the "icebox" class. Icebox size watermelons are ideal for small families, since the fruits do not grow too large — they will fit into the refrigerator with ease.

Watermelons make a delicious dessert if they are soaked in a brandy or whisky liqueur for several hours and then served with ice-cream.

Perhaps the most difficult part of growing watermelons is telling when they are ripe. During a trip to Taiwan visiting China's leading watermelon breeder,

I was told of a foolproof method to test a watermelon for ripeness. It consists of rapping the fruit with your knuckle. If it sounds like rapping your forehead, the watermelon is not yet ripe; if it sounds like your Adam's apple or chest it's ripe; and if it sounds like your stomach, it's over-ripe.

Strips of black plastic mulch will produce earlier fruit and healthier vines by conserving moisture, keeping down weeds and maintaining a warm soil temperature.

Pictured above in early summer is one of the most beautiful of Colonial herb gardens. Located at Pennsbury Manor, near Philadelphia, it was created by William Penn who was himself a keen gardener.

HERBS
A Top Ten Selection

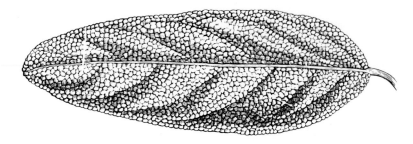

Sage leaf, shown here, has a delightful spicy fragrance. It adds good flavor to many meat dishes and stews.

In colonial days a herb garden was considered almost a necessity of life, providing flavors for the kitchen, fragrance during winter and medicine in times of ailment.

One of the big problems concerning herbs is how to grow them effectively without making your garden seem as though it is filled with a bunch of weeds, since many of the most popular herbs do indeed resemble vigorous clumps of weeds.

The main point to realize with herbs is that you do not need a lot of plants to provide sufficient spices for the average family, and it is often sufficient to tuck a plant or two in between shrubs, in corners of a rockery and other odd spots around the garden. Many kinds of herbs will grow easily in pots, and one of the most original herb garden ideas is to plant them between the spokes of a wagon wheel set into the ground. Don't try growing herbs in rows. That's terribly wasteful, even though a packet of herb seeds contains enough for hundreds — even thousands of plants. A better method is to grow them in groups of clumps — each with its own private bed the size of a seed flat approximately 31 by 17 in. In fact it's a good idea to knock the bottom out of some old seed flats and sink them in the soil to provide your herb bed, and help to keep the herbs within bounds.

Many herbs can be direct-sown into the garden, but since a few plants go a long way, they are best started indoors in Jiffy-7 pellets and transplanted.

Here's a guide to growing what I would consider to be the ten most popular and most useful of all herbs:

Parsley — Use as a garnish on meats, salads, egg dishes, soups, sandwiches, fish and potatoes. Parsley is king of herbs and high in nutritional value.

Always soak the seed for 24 hours in warm water before sowing either directly into the garden or in Jiffy-7 peat pellets for transplanting. Otherwise it can be one of the slowest seeds to germinate. Sow the seeds outdoors about three weeks before the last frost date in your area. Apart from knowing the trick about speedy germination there is little else to know about growing parsley. It seems to thrive under a wide variety of soil and climate conditions.

Mature plants are extremely hardy, and in most areas plants will stay productive into December. If a straw mulch is applied for protection after that it will yield even longer, since it is a biennial and will not go to seed until the second season.

Make one sowing early for summer and fall harvest, and another small sowing in July to obtain young plants for transplanting to pots for growing indoors in a sunny window. Sow seed in rows 1/2 in. deep, and thin seedlings to six in. apart. A packet of seeds normally plants a 30 ft. row, but for a family of four, a 5 ft. row is plenty.

Parsley is at home in a flower bed, especially as a decorative edging. Plain and curly-leafed varieties are sold, but the curly-leaf kind is by far the most popular. Planted in a wire basket, parsley can make a magnificent hanging basket, providing it has 6 hours sunlight each day.

Chives — A spring salad without chives is like a lamb chop without mint sauce. In the garden chives are such a vigorous hardy perennial you will need to divide up clumps every other year to stop them going wild. They grow easily from seed, sown directly into the garden or into containers 1/4 in. deep. The hollow stems will be ready to pick in about 80 days for dicing to add a mild onion flavor to salads, soups, stews, cheese sauces and potatoes. In early summer they often produce clumps of cheerful pink flowers, and if you pot-up a few plants in the fall, you can grow them indoors on a sunny window sill to provide fresh pickings during winter. Two or three healthy clumps is all you'll need.

Sage — Said to soothe the nerves, the dried leaves of sage add essential flavor to stuffings for pork, chicken, turkey, duck or goose. Plant sage seeds 1/4 in. deep in a sunny part of your garden. Five or six plants is ample for a family of four. They grow quickly and produce gray oval leaves which are pleasantly fragrant. Plants will last several years, and reseed themselves easily.

Mint — If parsley is the king of herbs then mint is surely queen. She is loved for her exquisite flavor and fragrance. Breathing her crushed leaves is said to clear the sinuses and arouse the senses. In drinks her refreshing taste is matchless — witness the mint julep, creme de menthe and mint-flavored ice tea. Mint sauce, made simply from chopped mint leaves and vinegar, is great to flavor lamb and new potatoes or baby carrots. Once you have mint in your garden you're never likely to be without it. Since mint spreads so rapidly it is best to plant the roots or seeds in a sunken container to keep it within limits. Although spearmint is the most popular variety grown, applemint and catmint are good varieties, and they can be grown as house plants.

Fennel — The fleshy leaf base of fennel has a strong anise flavor. It is eaten like celery, or chopped to flavor salads. The leaf stalks are also delicious when cooked as a vegetable. Use the fresh or dried leaves for fennel tea, and sprinkle seeds in soup to add a strong flavor. Fennel grows rapidly as an annual from seed, prefers a sunny location and cool growing conditions. Sow seed directly into the garden 1/4 in. deep, thinning seedlings to 12 ins. apart.

Thyme — This hardy perennial makes a fast growing ground cover. Liking sun, good drainage, and tolerant of dry weather, it is a rugged, reliable herb that bears lovely lavender-colored flowers and tiny aromatic leaves. These leaves are used to flavor meat loaf, soups, stews, casseroles, sauces and poultry. Start from seed, sow in rows directly into the garden in early spring or — better still — scrounge some root divisions from a gardening friend. Three plants are plenty for the average family.

Dill — A tall growing plant with feathery foliage and yellow umbel shaped flower heads. Start plants from seed in early spring, choosing a sunny location. Sow seed 1/4 in. deep in rows, thinning plants to stand 12 ins. apart. Although dill is really an annual, it self sows like a weed, so once you have a plant you're likely to have dill around for a long time. Both the leaves and seeds are used for flavoring pickles, and the chopped leaves, used with restraint, are good in soups, stews, sauces and fish dishes. Six plants is ample.

Sweet Marjoram — Plants of sweet marjoram form a thick dense growth, producing masses of small, fragrant velvety leaves and tiny pink flowers. The leaves are used fresh or dried to season poultry dressings, soups, salads, sauces and fish dishes. Seed is sometimes slow to germinate, and best results will come from starting seeds indoors in Jiffy-7 peat pellets, transplanting the seedlings into the garden after danger of frost. In sheltered locations sweet marjoram will winter over. One or two clumps is adequate for normal demands.

Basil — Sweet basil has lovely green leaves, scented like cloves. Used sparingly, they impart a delicious flavor to tomato dishes, salads, omelettes, sausages and cooked meats. A purple-colored variety called *Ornamental Basil* is equally useful as a herb, and additionally useful as a border planting around flower beds. Start seed of both varieties indoors in Jiffy-7 peat pellets and set out young plants in a sunny location, or direct sow into the garden after danger of frost. A group of six to ten plants is plenty.

Rosemary — Choosing the tenth most popular and most useful herb is difficult because so many herbs could qualify — horehound, summer savory and lavender to mention just a few. Rosemary gets my vote because it is so important in good cooking as a flavor additive. The leaves should be used sparingly to flavor meats, sauces and soups. In colonial days a tea made from rosemary was brewed for winter refreshment and the relief of colds. A half-hardy perennial, it takes about 85 days to mature from seed, likes a sunny location and good drainage. Planted in a large pot, it can be wintered over as a house plant. Start seed in Jiffy-7 peat pellets and transplant after your last frost date. Plants soon develop into bushy clumps, and one or two of these is sufficient for normal needs.

Half the value of growing herbs is drying them. Dried herbs will keep indefinitely, and many are decorative.

The quicker the drying process, the more flavorful the herbs will be. Chop stems and leaves and store them in air-tight jars. Store herb seeds until ready to use, then crush them to a powder with a pestle or rolling pin.

(*Left*) *Flower heads of Sweet Marjoram.*

(*Right*) *Clump of Thyme in full bloom.*

(*Left*) *Parsley growing indoors.*

(*Right*) *Row of Sage creating a low hedge.*

(*Left*) *Flowers and stems of Chives are edible.*

(*Right*) *Flower head of Fennel resembles Dill.*

81

BERRIES & SMALL FRUITS

By careful selection it's possible to have a succession of delectable berries coming into fruit from spring until fall, starting with early strawberries and raspberries, followed by bilberries and gooseberries, blackberries and loganberries, wine berries, blueberries, cranberries, and fall raspberries.

The temptation to grow berries is so great that the problem is generally one of space and selection.

In alphabetical order, following are the most widely grown and practical kinds.

Blackberry. (Also Loganberry and Boysenberry) Wild blackberries grow with such abandon throughout the waysides of America, many people might see little point to cultivate them in their own yard. But, if you live in an area where they are the least bit scarce it makes good sense to grow your own.

Eaten fresh as a dessert, or made into famous blackberry cobbler pie and jams, they have a wild flavor that no artificial flavor can possibly match.

Loganberries and boysenberries are blackberry hybrids, and their culture is identical.

Although blackberries are more commonly seen as a tangle of brambles, in the garden they can be grown tidily like raspberries on wire supports and pruned to several strong canes.

They are normally bought as healthy root stocks, and need planting in spring or fall 4 feet apart three inches deep in fertile soil enriched with garden compost or decomposed animal manures. Since some varieties are self-sterile, it is best to plant two varieties for successful pollination and adequate yields.

Like thornless roses, there are thornless blackberries, and instead of rambling vines that need support to keep within bounds there are sturdy dwarf varieties, of which *Darrow* is the most notable.

Vigorous pruning is needed to keep them tidy and easily accessible. When new shoots reach several feet in height tops can be pruned to encourage side branches. The previous season's growth produces fruit, so allow new shoots to develop. After fruiting cut back all the old canes and thin new shoots to about 12 good canes for berry-bearing the next season. The rambling type can be spread out like a fan on wires, while the bush kinds can be trimmed of side shoots to make a tidy plant.

You can't always tell a ripe blackberry by color. If you have to tug on a blackberry to remove it from the vine, it is not ripe. Ripe blackberries will fall off into your hand at the slightest touch.

Blueberry. About the only serious problem with blueberries is the bird population. They relish the luscious fruit, and a flock of starlings will make short work of a whole bush-load of ripe berries, which is why you often see them grown in special bird-proof cages.

Blueberries are one of the few fruits that will tolerate light shade, and they *do* prefer an acid soil. They also serve well as a fruiting hedge, creating an inpenetrable barrier loaded with fruit in summer.

Planting of roots or rooted cuttings can be done in spring or fall in a fertile, well-drained soil enriched with soil conditioner such as peat moss, garden compost or animal manures. Two-year old roots will bear well in three years.

They are not self-pollinating and two different varieties are needed for successful pollination.

Fruit will ripen in clusters over a period of two months.

Pruning is done in winter or early spring to cut away any weak or dead branches.

Feed each spring with fertilizers formulated for "acid loving plants."

Gooseberries and Currants. Owing to the fact that they are carriers of rust disease affecting pine trees, the growing of both red currants and gooseberries is restricted in certain states.

If the growing of these were ever restricted in England, however, you would probably see a national uprising. The gooseberry is such a favored fruit among Englishmen that they even have gooseberry-growing contests where specimens the size of golf-balls are not uncommon.

Gooseberries have a reputation for "tartness," but this is entirely undeserving, since a ripe gooseberry has a flavor as sweet as any grape. The problem is that people insist on picking gooseberries before they are fully ripe. With green gooseberries it's a little hard to tell because they stay green even when ripe, but a ripe gooseberry feels soft and not hard. There are red varieties which are also generally available. They make fabulous pies and jams, and are good for canning.

Two-year old plants should be set into the garden in spring or fall, in an open, sunny location spaced four feet apart. They tolerate a wide-range of soil conditions, as long as it is fertile and enriched with garden compost or animal manures, and will start to bear fruit as soon as they are established, although decent yields will take a minimum of two years after planting.

Propagation is possible from cuttings in summer or layering — by pegging a branch into the soil until it takes root.

Neither currants nor gooseberries like hot summers, and will do best in areas where they can flower and fruit during cool weather. A heavy mulch around the roots will help to keep soil cool and moist.

Raspberries. The big question about raspberries concerns flavor. Are the red, black or yellow varieties better tasting? The less familiar black and yellow varieties are certainly intriguing, and really it's all a matter of personal preference, but in my own opinion it is still the red kinds that win my vote. Certainly, the red variety is still the most widely grown, of which, there are summer-bearing, fall-bearing, and "everbearing."

(*Above left*) *Black French hybrid grape, Baco Noire is an excellent wine grape, with a tartly-sweet flavor when eaten fresh.*

(*Top right*) *Red variety of gooseberry. Makes the finest jelly.*

(*Center*) *Red currants have high vitamin C content.*

(*Above*) *Wine berries growing wild, and ready for picking.*

(*Right*) *Black raspberries bear abundantly in early summer.*

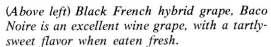

Unquestionably, the best of the "everbearing" kinds is a new variety called *Heritage* which produces a moderate crop of large red berries on old canes in early summer, followed by a blockbuster yield on new canes in fall.

Year old, virus-free roots can be planted in spring or fall spaced two feet apart and sandwiched between wire supports to hold the canes erect and tidy.

Once established, raspberries will throw up countless suckers, and for maximum productivity all but six to eight new canes should be thinned out. Cut out old fruited canes to ground level and destroy all dead or broken canes.

Soil with plenty of garden compost and well-rotted leaf mold or animal manure is best, and a regular feeding of vegetable fertilizer each spring will ensure plump well developed fruit.

Strawberries (see p. 69)

Wine Berries. A bramble native to the Orient, wine berries are not often seen in home gardens, but they grow with wild abandon in hedgerows throughout the United States. Few other plants have naturalized so successfully, and in mid-summer they provide easy picking.

The arching canes bear hairy red buds that are slightly sticky on touch, and open out to reveal the bright red raspberry-shaped fruit at the peak of ripeness.

Makes delicious wines and jams, and is good eaten fresh provided it is picked when fully ripe. The test for ripeness is when the berry falls into your hand at the slightest touch.

Layering is an easy means of propagation. Just peg a cane into the soil and let it root by itself. Then prune away the cane from the parent plant, and leave the rooted portion for use as a transplant.

Grapes. One of the most uplifting sights in nature is to wander through a wine-making district in late summer or early fall and catch the heady fragrance of ripened grapes growing tier-upon-tier along the hillsides.

Although California's Napa Valley claims to be one of the richest wine-growing areas of the world, for me nothing can equal the Finger Lakes region of New York State where freshly baked grape pies are sold at roadside stands, and the threat of early frost lingers in the air even as the pickers strip the vines in their annual race against time.

Red, white and dusky black grapes hang in gorgeous clumps, and a surge of enthusiasm fills the mind and body with one dominating purpose — *to plant grapes* — to emulate Ulysses and Bacchus of Greek mythology with a veritable feast of vine-ripened grapes for gorging fresh, fermenting as wine, and transforming into delectable jams and pies.

In recent years nurserymen have begun to offer a new series of wine grapes called French Hybrids. These originated by crossing the sophisticated European varieties with hardy, disease-resistant American varieties, to create a reliable selection of wine grapes for American conditions. They are proving slow to catch on, but that is always the case with new fruits. The very finest of these in my opinion is *Baco Noire* producing abundant clusters of tartly-sweet grapes that gleam like black pearls when growing on the vine.

It's still the old-fashioned stand-bys that remain favorites as dessert grapes, and these include *Catawba* (red), *Concord* (black), *Niagara* (white), and *Seedless Interlaken* (amber). They all make satisfactory wines as well.

There are many local favorites too numerous to name, such as the muscadine, of the South, and again it is wise to check with the local extension service if you are in doubt about adaptability.

Growing grapes is easy. They like a sunny, open position, and should be trained up a wire fence, trellis, or arbor for support. Rooted cuttings and two-year old roots can be bought in spring or fall from many local garden centers and mail order catalogs. Most are self-pollinating, but it's always best to have more than one variety. At least three years are needed for vines to reach peak productivity.

Although grapes will tolerate a wide range of soil conditions they favor a dry, sandy fertile soil enriched with garden compost or well-decomposed animal manure.

Pruning is the secret to abundant yields, and this should be done in early spring before new growth begins. The idea of pruning is to keep a compact, airy vine with a limited number of growing points for maximum fruit formation

Grapes can be propagated from ground layering or cuttings. With ground layering you simply bend a vine so it touches good soil and is buried at a leaf joint by anchoring with a notched peg. Roots will form in summer so that the rest of the vine can be cut away to leave a healthy transplant. Cuttings can be made by taking a six inch length of vine with leaf buds in early spring, dipping in a root hormone, and setting into containers filled with planting soil.

Dwarf Fruit Trees

These Minis Are Here to Stay

In the world of home gardening, minis are in fashion. Dwarf flowers are in fashion — they bloom earlier, produce more flowers, fewer leaves and don't blow over in the wind. Dwarf vegetables are in fashion — they take up less space and don't need poles for support.

Dwarf fruit trees especially are in fashion. They bear fruit sooner; they are easier to prune, easier to spray and easier to pick. They are revolutionizing home fruit tree gardens.

An area no larger than your living room is ample for a mini-grove of apples, pears, black plums and peaches. The little trees are fine for small city and town lots. And apartment dwellers needn't feel left out either — at least one variety of peach tree (*Bonanza*) and a new nectarine (*Nectarina*) will grow in tubs on a sunny balcony or patio, producing blossoms in Spring and excellent quality fruit in late Summer.

Most dwarf fruit trees are not naturally dwarf. They are man-made, usually by grafting normal fruit trees onto a special root system that keeps the rest of the tree dwarf. You can see where the graft was made — it's the swollen area towards the base of the trunk. When planting, you must keep this graft above soil level, otherwise it will produce roots of the wrong type and destroy the dwarfing effect. Some fruit trees cannot bear fruit unless pollinated by another variety. Apricots, nectarines, sour cherries, European plums and peaches are mostly self-fruitful and don't require cross pollination. But apples, pears, sweet cherries and Japanese plums need two varieties to bear fruit.

This explains one reason for the popularity of combination fruit trees — particularly apples and pears — where up to five varieties are grafted onto the same tree. Each grafted variety will pollinate another, and the result is a tree with several different apples or pears growing on it.

If you have a neighbor with fruit trees (dwarf or tall) his trees will pollinate yours.

Selection of varieties depends on personal preference and availability. *Stanley Dwarf* plum is normally the heaviest bearing plum variety. *Red Delicious* and *Yellow Delicious* apples make a perfect match, and the pears *Bartlett* and *Clapp's Favorite* are good companions. Dwarf sweet cherries are still in the making and most nurseries cannot yet offer much of a choice. Among the best peaches are *Bonanza*, a natural dwarf, that's extra neat and compact, and *Hale Haven*, a large yellow-fleshed freestone fine for eating fresh and canned.

Fall or spring are perfect times to begin your mini-orchard.

Your dwarf fruit trees will usually bear fruit the second year after planting, provided they are fed each year with an application of shrub and tree fertilizer, and pruned to a tidy shape.

85

How to Plant a Dwarf Fruit Tree

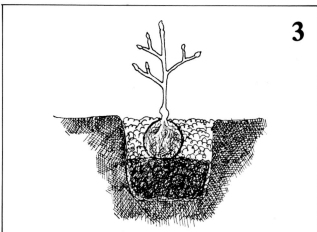

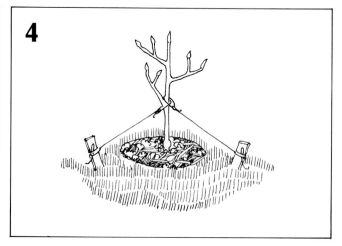

The most successful way to plant a dwarf fruit tree is to buy one "balled and burlapped". They cost more than bare-root trees, but they are almost idiot-proof. They have been dug from the nursery with a good-size root ball and then wrapped in burlap sacking to keep the soil well packed around the roots.

Take your tree home and then follow these steps:
1 — Dig a hole where you want the tree to grow in a sunny, well-drained location. Make the hole at least twice the depth of the root ball and twice the width.
2 — Carefully unwrap the root-ball, disturbing as little soil as necessary around the roots. Fill the hole to half its depth with a mixture of good garden top-soil, garden compost and peat moss. Pour a bucket of water over this and set the tree so the top of the root ball is level with the top of the hole.
3 — Keeping the tree centered in the hole, fill the top half of the hole with a mixture of garden soil and peat moss and a tree fertilizer. Pour in another bucket of water and tread the soil down firmly, leaving 1 inch lip around the edge to catch water.

4 — If the tree is in an exposed position, support it with guide ropes and pegs, cushioning the area attached to the trunk with rubber tubing or paper wadding to protect the bark from damage.

Dwarf fruit trees have a swelling at the base of the trunk where they were grafted onto a dwarf root stock at an early age. This swollen portion must not come in contact with the soil, otherwise it may grow roots that will destroy the dwarfing effect.

Fruit trees you buy through the mail are normally bare-root, and require a little extra care in handling. Follow the same planting procedure, digging a generous hole, but before planting soak the roots in water for at least half a day. Trim off any broken roots and prune the tree to a tidy shape if necessary.

Biggest losses with newly planted fruit trees are from dehydration, so keep the tree watered, especially if a dry, windy spell follows planting. Although most fruit trees are planted in spring, they have an equal chance of success from a fall planting. Don't allow grass to grow up to the trunk, and keep weeds down with a decorative light mulch such as bark or cocoa hulls.

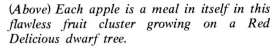

(*Above*) *Each apple is a meal in itself in this flawless fruit cluster growing on a Red Delicious dwarf tree.*

(*Top, left*) *Yields like this from a dwarf Golden Delicious apple tree are possible by a regular spraying program and twice-yearly fertilizer applications in spring and fall.*

(*Above*) *Dwarf fruit trees like this Elberta peach bear regular size fruit and are easier to pick. Regular spray program and fertilizer applications assure this abundance and quality.*

(*Top, right*) *Large pale lemon yellow fruit are typical of Clapp's Favorite, a widely available dwarf pear with a crisp juicy dessert flavor.*

Nut Trees
for Home Gardens

There's something primeval about nut trees. Before man evolved from an ape, nuts probably formed a food staple that modern man still finds hard to resist, and the pleasure of finding a nut tree in the wild is akin to the feeling of finding buried treasure.

For moderate size yards that beg to be planted with trees, nut trees offer several benefits — sturdy hard-wood growth that lasts a long time and resists wind damage, a rich canopy of leaves in summer, giving dense shade and a bountiful supply of delicious nuts. Fertilizers high in phosphorus are the key to successful nut production.

Nut trees come in all shapes and sizes, and there's something to suit every situation.

The majestic American chestnut is all but extinct, except for a few isolated pockets free of the dreaded blight disease which swept America, and a few saplings which still cling to life, but will succumb to the disease in time.

Thanks to the United States Department of Agriculture, the susceptible American chestnut has been replaced with a hardy, disease-resistant kind called the Chinese chestnut (Castanea dentata). It is not as sturdy or grand as the American chestnut but it does have a lot to recommend it. In form, it has a dense spreading, rounded shape with branches starting close to the ground from a single trunk. Allow at least 40 feet between trees, and plant two for reliable nut production, starting to bear within three or four years of transplanting.

Beautiful panicles of white blossoms appear in early summer, and are ornamental when seen from a distance. They give off a strong scent which some people find unpleasant, but it lasts only a week or two. The nuts are formed in September depending on location, and are contained in prickly cases in groups. When ripe the cases split and eject the handsome brown nuts. As a general rule, it will do well wherever peaches can be grown.

Almonds are closely related to peaches, and in appearance they look like a peach tree. Hall's hardy almond is a highly recommended variety because it is reliable even in the north, bears a good crop of delicious, thin shelled nuts, and is highly ornamental during spring with masses of pink flowers. Plant two or more trees for best results. Peach and nectarine trees can also act as pollinators.

Hazelnuts (or filberts) grow more like a shrub than a tree, and indeed a hazelnut hedge is a practical idea. Under normal conditions many thin branches spring from ground level and reach a height of eight to ten feet. If you prefer a tree form habit the suckers and side shoots can be pruned away as they sprout leaving one central branch to form the trunk. Tree forms will grow to 15 feet. At least two varieties are needed for pollination, and one of these should be a variety called "Barcelona." Crops can be expected the second or third year after planting.

The most respected of all nut trees is the Black Walnut (Juglans nigra) which is highly valued for its rock-hard, decorative wood. A slow-growing tree capable of growing to 150 ft., it has two annoying habits which even homeowners should realize before rushing out to plant them for investment value and nut production.

First, it is a "messy tree." The nuts are enclosed in green hulls which drop and turn coal-black when ripe. On a driveway they can be a nuisance, and on a lawn they create havoc. Close to a vegetable garden the rambling root system will give off a toxin which stunts growth of vegetables. Leaf-drop is annoyingly early, leaving a stark, bare tree devoid of any fall color. Planted in a wild hedgerow or near a meadow, they are fine, but unless you grow a special commercial variety called Thomas black walnut the tough shells will be too much trouble. Thomas black walnuts are thin-shelled nuts, and the best variety for home gardens.

Closely related to the black walnut is the Butternut (Juglans cineria), and once you have tasted butternuts you will swear it is the best-flavored nut of all. The nuts are oval, shaped like elongated black walnuts, and the shells are hard, but the meaty interior is worth all the trouble of getting to them. Grows to 90 ft. or more.

The Carpathian strain of English walnut has become a popular hardy nut tree, and valuable for shade. The nuts are easy to crack, and will start to bear four to seven years after planting.

Pecan trees (Carya pecan) are usually associated with the South, but new Northern varieties developed in Illinois have extended the range even into New York State. They are related to hickories and can be pollinated by hickories for nut production. Nuts from northern pecans are not as large as the southern types, and the shells are not as thin, but the flavor is identical, and since these trees will reach a height of over 50 feet when full grown they need plenty of room, allowing at least 40 ft. between trees.

The Hickory (Carya laciniosa) is one of the richest-colored trees in fall, creating brilliant yellow and orange colors that almost dazzle the eye. Varieties sold by nurseries are thinner-shelled than the wild hickories, and less of a nuisance to crack. Hickory wood is a delight to burn, imparting a fragrance so good that it is used extensively to flavor smoked hams.

Nut trees are not difficult to grow, requiring an open sunny location to get established, and good drainage, although they like a moist soil, and in the wild grow extensively along creeks and river banks. A deep, fertile soil is best, and it's always a wise precaution to check with your local state extension service for bulletins and advice about growing nut trees in your particular area.

(*Above*) English walnuts are a misnomer, since the most widely grown hardy variety actually comes from Persia.

(*Top left*) Chinese chestnuts splitting open and ejecting the ripe, brown nuts.

(*Top*) Almonds grow wherever peaches succeed.

(*Center*) Hazelnuts, or filberts, can be grown as a hedge.

(*Left*) Black walnuts, showing green and black outer hulls, inner shell case and edible nuts.

Canning, Freezing & Dry Storage

For best results from both canning and freezing home grown vegetables it is essential to use only young, fresh, unblemished produce completely free of disease or discoloration. Pickings made in the morning are best, and it is essential to keep the time from harvesting to preparation at a minimum.

All vegetables need to be scalded or blanched in boiling water. This inactivates certain enzymes present in plant cells, and ensures that the color, flavor and nutritional value are retained during prolonged periods of storage.

A wire basket that fits inside a large pan is best for blanching, filling the pan with 6 pints of water for every pound of prepared vegetables, and bring to the boil. Immerse the basket of fresh vegetables into the already boiling water and cook for the recommended length of time. Then steep the basket of cooked vegetables quickly into cold water to chill. Drain thoroughly and dry on absorbent paper towels. The same water can be used six times before changing·

Freezing Fruits & Vegetables

Freezing home-grown food is the fastest, most convenient method of preserving. Unfortunately, a freezer demands a significant investment, and a small garden is not likely to yield sufficient surplus crops to fill a freezer. However, in-season produce is often inexpensive, and it's often possible to buy fresh vegetables in season at bargain rates, especially beans, tomatoes and corn.

Frozen produce must be packed in airtight containers with close fitting lids or plastic bags that can be sealed. With these available, the procedure for freezing is simple. For example:

Strawberries (also raspberries, blackberries and other small fruits)

Select firm, ripe berries. You'll need 2/3 quart to make one pint frozen. Wash berries in cold water and drain. Remove stems and slice the berries into a bowl. Sprinkle sugar over the berries (3/4 cup to each quart of berries). Turn berries over until sugar is evenly dissolved and juice is formed.

Pack berries into a rigid plastic container or plastic bag. Seal so these are watertight. Then freeze and store at zero degrees or below until ready for serving. The berries can also be packed without sweetening, with sugar added at time of serving.

Other good garden products to freeze are shown in the following table.

VEGETABLE	PREPARATION PRIOR TO FREEZING	BOILING TIME IN MINUTES
Asparagus	Sort stalks according to thickness. Wash. Cut into 2-inch lengths. **Boil. Chill. Drain.** Pack, leaving no head space.	Small 2 Large 4
Beans, Lima	Shell. Wash. **Boil. Chill. Drain.**	Small 2 Large 4
Beans, Snap	Wash. Cut into 2-inch lengths. **Boil. Chill. Drain.**	3
Beets	Wash. Trim tops, leaving ½ inch of stems. Boil until tender. **Chill.** Peel and cut into quarters. **Drain.**	Small 30
Broccoli	Wash, peel stalks, and cut into pieces 1-inch across. To remove insects, soak for ½ hour in salt-water (4 tsp. salt, 1 gallon cold water). Split lengthwise. **Boil. Chill. Drain.** Pack, leaving no head space.	3
Brussels Sprouts	Remove loose outer leaves. Wash. **Boil. Chill. Drain.** Pack, leaving no head space.	Small 3 Large 5
Carrots	Remove tops. Wash and peel. Leave small carrots whole. Cut others into slices or cubes. **Boil. Chill. Drain.**	Whole 5 Cut 2
Cauliflower	Wash and cut into pieces 1-inch across. To remove insects, soak for ½ hour in salt-water (4 tsp. salt, 1 gallon cold water). Drain. **Boil** in salt-water (4 tsp. salt, 1 gallon water). **Chill.** Pack, leaving no head space.	3
Corn, Whole-kernel	Husk, remove silks and wash. **Boil. Chill. Drain.** Cut kernels from cob.	4
On-the-cob	Husk, silk and wash. Sort according to size. **Boil. Chill. Drain.**	Small 7 Large 11
Greens, All Kinds	Wash. Remove tough stems and diseased or blemished leaves. **Boil. Chill. Drain.**	2-3
Kohl-rabi	Remove tops and roots. Wash, peel, cut into slices or cubes. **Boil. Chill. Drain.**	1
Okra	Wash. Remove stems. **Boil. Chill. Drain.**	3-4
Parsnips	Remove tops. Wash, peel, cut into slices or cubes. **Boil. Chill. Drain.**	2
Peas	Shell. **Boil. Chill. Drain.**	1½-2
Rhubarb	Wash and peel stems. Cut into 2 in. pieces. **Boil. Chill. Drain.**	1
Rutabagas and Turnips	Remove tops. Wash, peel, cut into cubes. **Boil. Chill. Drain.**	2
Squash, Winter and Pumpkin	Wash. Cut into pieces. Remove seeds. Cook until tender. Remove rind. Put pulp through sieve. Cool by placing pan containing puree into cold water. Stir to speed chilling.	until tender

If you live 5,000 feet or more above sea level, boil 1 minute longer than time specified.

How to Can Tomatoes and Beans

With today's cost of food so high, there is more reason than ever to consider canning garden-fresh vegetables.

Some of the most worthwhile vegetables to can include tomatoes, beans, beets, broccoli, Brussels sprouts, carrots, cauliflower, peas, pepper and zucchini squash.

The most widely canned vegetables are tomatoes and beans. Here are some hints on canning these successfully:

Tomatoes

Choose only fresh, firm ripe tomatoes. Those with decayed spots or cracks are unfit for canning. Wash and drain enough tomatoes for one canner load. Place tomatoes in a wire basket or cheesecloth and submerge in boiling water about 1/2 minute to loosen skins.

Then dip into cold water and drain. Next, cut out all cores, remove skins and trim off any green spots. Cut tomatoes into quarters or leave whole.

Fill hot canning jars, adding 1 teaspoon of salt per quart, and filling air spaces with juice. Run a table knife between tomatoes and sides of jar to release any air bubbles. Wipe the mouth clean, then seal tightly with lid and screw band. As each jar is filled stand it in a canner of hot water, covering jars 1 to 2 inches. Place cover on canner, bring to boil and leave for 45 minutes in the case of quart jars (35 minutes for pints) at elevations less than 1000 feet above sea level. Remove jars from canner, and let cool for 12 hours. To test for a successful seal remove the screw band, and press down in the center of the lid. If lid stays depressed, jar is sealed. Store the jars, without the bands, in a cool, dark place.

Beans

Thoroughly wash freshly gathered beans, which must be young, tender and crisp, then drain. Trim the ends, remove any strings, and cut beans into pieces. Cover the beans with boiling water and boil for 5 minutes, or pack raw into a heated pint or quart jar. Add 1 teaspoon of salt per quart, and cover beans with boiling water. Wipe top of jar clean, then seal with lid and screw band.

Put jars into a steam-pressure canner containing 2-3 inches of hot water, place canner over heat, and lock cover. Leave canner vent open to allow steam to escape for 10 minutes, then close vent. At elevations less than 2000 feet above sea level keep pressure steady at 10 pounds for 25 minutes in the case of quarts (20 minutes for pints). Stand jars to cool for 12 hours, and test for a successful seal by removing the screw band and pressing down in the center of the lid. If lid stays depressed, jar is sealed. Store jars without the bands in a cool place. Before tasting, bring the beans to a boil and simmer for ten minutes.

Shown above are two stages in canning beans and tomatoes. Top picture shows sealing a jar of beans with a screw band, while the bottom picture shows whole unblemished tomatoes being washed for a canner load.

91

Storage of Vegetables

In Colonial days before canning and freezing were invented, vegetables were stored over winter in "root cellars". This was generally a room below ground with stone walls and a dirt floor, with ventilation provided by a pipe or shaft.

Root crops such as carrots, beets, turnips, potatoes, parsnips and onions were then stored and kept indefinitely for winter consumption. Basements in homes can provide similar keeping conditions for vegetables, and certain fruits. Here are some of the more useful.

VEGETABLE	HOW TO STORE
Beans, Lima	Air dry pods. Shell. Store in bags in dry cupboard.
Beans, Shelled	Air dry pods. Shell. Store in bags in dry cupboard.
Beets	Clean away soil. Remove tops. Store in box of moist sand in cool basement. Best temperature range is 35-40° F.
Carrots	Clean away soil. Remove tops. Store in box of moist sand in cool basement. Best temperature range is 35-40° F.
Onions	Clean away soil. Store in shallow boxes or hang from strings in cool dry basement. Best temperature range is 50-60° F.
Parsnips	Clean away soil. Store in box of moist sand in a cool basement. Best temperature range is 35-40° F.
Peanuts	Shell. Air dry. Roast.
Potatoes	Clean away soil. Store in sacks in cool basement. Best temperature range is 35-40° F.
Salsify	Clean away soil. Store in box of moist sand in cool basement. Best temperature range is 35-40° F.
Squash, Winter	Store on shelves in cool dry basement. Best temperature range is 50 to 60° F.
Tomatoes	Pick green. Will ripen indoors in light or dark over period of several weeks.
Turnips	Clean away soil. Store in box of moist sand in cool basement. Best temperature range is 35-40° F.
Apples & Pears	Store as close to 32° F as possible in a moist atmosphere.

Vegetables to Winter Over in Your Garden

There is a select group of popular vegetables which are unusually hardy, and will survive well into winter (if not all through winter) in most areas of the United States. During days when heavy snowfalls or freezing are predicted, heaping leaves or straw around the plants will often give them sufficient protection to pull through the winter.

VEGETABLE	REMARKS
Brussels sprouts	Extremely hardy. Will survive to Christmas and even later.
Chard	Extremely hardy. Will survive to Christmas and later if protected with mulch on freezing nights.
Kale	Extremely hardy. Will survive to Christmas and later if protected with mulch on freezing nights.
Lettuce	Will grow all through winter if protected in a cold frame.
Parsley	Extremely hardy. During freezing cold nights heap mulch up around plants.
Parsnips	Extremely hardy. Can be pulled from ground all through winter if ground kept from freezing by a thick layer of mulch.
Spinach	Extremely hardy. During freezing nights protect plants with mulch.

Vegetables to Grow Indoors Over Winter

Even if all you have is a kitchen window there are a few worthwhile vegetables that can be grown to provide flavorful "greens" and garnish for soups, sandwiches and egg dishes.

Even the smallest kitchen window will generally have room for a selection of herbs - especially parsley, chives and thyme. A healthy clump of each will provide enough sprigs for a family of four all winter.

If a north window is all you have don't despair - garden cress, mustard and mung beans will fill your windows with vitamin-rich flavorful greenery. Once you add water to these three you can't **stop** them from germinating. Sow them all in produce trays filled with moist paper tissues. The mung beans will be ready in just a few days, while the garden cress and mustard will be ready for cutting in ten.

(*Top, right*) *Winesap apples are better for storage in a cool, humid atmosphere.*

(*Center, right*) *Acorn Squash Table King is a good winter squash bearing large fruit.*

(*Below*) *Pixie Hybrid tomato will bear fruit during late winter and early spring months when longer day length encourages ripening.*

(*Above*) *Butternut squash is another good winter squash with better-than-average keeping qualities.*

(*Center left*) *Carrots keep over winter in moist sand in a cool basement*

(*Top, left*) *Oakleaf lettuce photographed in a cold frame outdoors in the dead of winter.*

93

How to Succeed at Community Gardening

Public opinion expert, George Gallup, Jr., president of the Gallup Organization, told the nation's leading seedsmen that according to a study called the National Garden Study, there are 30,000,000 people in America who would garden if they had the land.

Gallup also revealed that of these 30,000,000 who want to garden 18,000,000 said they would garden if land was made available to them in the form of "community gardens" whereby local authorities provide garden plots on a rental basis.

Gallup's survey was conducted during the months of July and August at the height of the vegetable growing season, with the objective of measuring the incidence of vegetable gardening.

How to Start a Community Garden

The most important requirement for any successful community garden project is a "leader" — someone with enthusiasm plus a gift for planning and organizing.

The next most important need is land, which can be obtained from community-minded companies, local planning authorities, church groups, public spirited private landowners and other sources.

The best location is within easy reach of the majority of participants, and with access to a water supply. Secure a location that is not "temporary." There's nothing more disheartening than to cultivate a piece of ground only to realize that it won't be available the following year.

Divide the land into equal size plots, and allocate one plot to each gardener or family group. Don't expect to garden the entire area like one big happy "commune." Each person with his own area to take care of and plant the way he wants is a better system.

Don't make the plots too large if you are mostly beginner gardeners. A small plot well cared for will yield more than a large area that is neglected.

Have everyone start on the same day. Pay for a farmer with a tractor to plow the ground or have all the plots roto-tilled at the same time. That gets everyone off to an enthusiastic start, and the experience of planting the seeds becomes pure joy. Leave room for pathways between plots.

Toilet facilities and a handy shed to lock up equipment should be taken into consideration.

In areas with potential vandalism it may be necessary to erect a fence, or ensure that the site located is not readily accessible to unauthorized personnel.

Youngsters Grow

Over 21,000 youthful gardeners in the Cleveland City School's youth garden program harvested more than $622,000 worth of fresh vegetables from an investment of $15,500, according to Peter J. Wotowiec, supervisor of the program.

What's more, these monetary figures include food value only. In addition to the fresh vegetables the youngsters raised nearly 20,000 bunches of flowers and indoor potted plants.

The Cleveland School Program originated in 1904 and includes tracts of land located throughout the city, where young people maintain individual garden plots. The total amount of space devoted to these tracts or "community gardens" exceeds 35 acres.

Those youngsters with garden space at home can still benefit from the program by enrolling for a home garden kit, distributed to participants at the proper planting time.

The program regards its monetary gains as only an incidental benefit, however. Far more important are the health and educational benefits and the impact on pupil development in the areas of environmental science, practical mathematics, social communication and career exploration, according to the supervisors.

This community gardening project run by the Cleveland Public Schools system is undoubtedly the largest of its kind anywhere in the world.

State Land Given

A national effort among governors of all states could make tremendous headway in establishing more community gardens in the United States, and one of the most farsighted programs is that being implemented by the state of Pennsylvania.

Governor Milton Shapp, of Pennsylvania, has launched a program turning over state land to create community gardens for people without garden space at home.

To accomplish this Governor Shapp appointed three members of his cabinet to make an inventory of state land and develop a working plan in time for spring planting.

In announcing his program to allot state land for vegetable gardens, Shapp noted that vacant lots and redevelopment areas where buildings have been torn down and not replaced, could provide inner-city residents with plots. Shapp's community garden plan also formed part of a presentation he made to the International Food Conference in Rome.

Communities Sponsor

In their first year of operation 175 employees grew vegetables and flowers on 120 plots, each measuring 20 ft. wide by 25 ft. deep, provided by RCA Laboratories, at

(Top, right) is a community garden in England where individual plot holders have constructed greenhouses.

(Center, right) These Washington D.C. youngsters are part of the District of Columbia youth garden program. Located at the National Arboretum, it is one of 65 planned, planted and maintained by children.

(Below, right) Gardening means family togetherness, an opportunity for parents and youngsters to share the benefits of outdoor exercise, and nutritional produce.

(Top, left) It's a good rule to allocate one plot per person when planning community gardens, but often two good friends like these can make a success of sharing a plot.

(Center, left) This employee at the David Sarnoff Research Center, Princeton, New Jersey, does some early chores on his plot in the RCA employee gardens project.

(Above, left) Two happy students in the Cleveland Public School system garden program.

the David Sarnoff Research Center, in Princeton, New Jersey. The part-time gardens proved so popular that the following year RCA set up 230 plots for 300 employees, and still had a waiting list of 25 workers.

This experience is typical of a number of progressive companies who are giving employees the opportunity to cultivate garden plots on spare company land.

Charles A. Hurford, industrial relations manager, at RCA, said that with vegetables in short supply and escalating food costs, employees had been diligent and no fair-weather gardeners who let the weeds take over had been found. "They come out here in the mornings, at lunch, after work and on weekends," he said, and went on to remark that the company gardeners represent a good cross section of their total staff, including laboratory directors and patent attorneys.

After employees requested the gardens, the facilities department plowed the plots and installed water pipes, while the employees formed their own three-man policing committee. The overall project was coordinated by the industrial relations department, which is willing to give other companies the benefit of its experience.

"We have a very imaginative group of people here," Hurford reported. "There have been some minor squabbles about the organic and insecticide philosophies, but a common front is put up against rabbits, groundhogs, and skunks who come out of the neighborhood woods to stalk the crop."

People without land of their own at home particularly like the idea of using garden space at work because it uses their travel time efficiently, allowing them to spend time on their gardens before and after working hours, and during breaks.

Community Gardens in Europe

The most famous community garden system in the world is undoubtedly that practiced in Great Britain, where tens of thousands of people rent garden plots from local authorities, corporations and nationalized industries in order to grow bountiful harvests of fresh vegetables and beautiful flowers.

In Britain these community or rental gardens are called "allotments," although there is a movement afoot to change the name officially to "leisure gardens" and to encourage more gardeners to landscape their plots with lawns and flowers. The British even have their own society of allotment gardeners called "The National Allotments and Gardens Society."

Great Britain presently has 57,303 acres of land under cultivation as community gardens, representing a total of 560,000 individual plots. These figures exclude Scotland and Northern Ireland.

Community gardens started in England during the Middle Ages. The coal mines, railways and industrial mills of the Industrial Revolution also encouraged community gardens as a benefit to employees. Today, the national coal mines and railways are still believed to be the largest providers of community gardens.

In 1806 legislation was started which eventually empowered local authorities to provide space for community gardens where even a small demand was shown to exist.

In Great Britain the average rental varies from a low of $2.00 per plot per year where no facilities whatsoever are provided, to a high of $20.00 where everything from a greenhouse, running water, all weather roads, a community center with toilets, and good fencing are provided.

It is also estimated that the British community gardeners are 99% men.

Community gardens like the British system are common throughout other European countries, particularly Germany, Holland and France, and an international conference on community gardens is held each year. In Amsterdam and Hamburg the concept of community gardens has reached its most advanced stage. Many not only have an area for growing vegetables, but they include lawns, flower beds, garden sculpture, espalier fruit trees and hedges, plus a small summerhouse for relaxing. Each garden is truly "a little bit of heaven."

How Not to Operate

Vegetable gardening requires a serious commitment on the part of an individual in order for that person to properly cultivate the soil, plant, and provide months of after care before the gardener reaps a harvest. To encourage individuals or families to plant gardens by inducements such as "give-away" programs, for example, is a big mistake, since that kind of practice stimulates too many potential "drop outs" who are likely to give up at the slightest excuse as soon as they realize that gardening needs hard work and careful attention.

It's also a big mistake to give away free seeds or free plants as an inducement to get people into a community gardening program. These commodities are not expensive, and it is no hardship for families to pay for these needs. In addition to the payment providing a necessary incentive to follow the job through, it allows people to make their own choice in the selection of varieties.

Freedom of choice in selecting precisely what you want to grow is part of the fun of gardening. Each person always prefers to choose named varieties, improved varieties, personal favorites or varieties adapted to his particular area or methods of cultivation. A vast portion of free seeds and plants are wasted on people who don't like the selection that is offered to them.

Remember that it is possible to force plants into bloom and into fruit by artificial means, but the natural growth is always better. So it is with good gardeners. Supervision, education, information and instruction — properly disseminated by a conscientious group leader — is worth far more in ensuring a successful community garden than all the free inducements in the world.